AF602143

THE GOOD WORK BOOK

How to enjoy your job & make it spiritually fulfilling

Suzie St George & Fiona McDougall

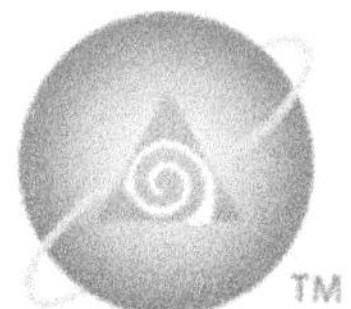

A Siramarti Publication

Revised Edition

Correspondence: enquiries@reachpotential.com.au

National Library of Australia Cataloguing-in-Publication entry
Creator: St George, Suzie, author
Title: The good work book : how to enjoy your job & make it spiritually fulfilling / Suzie St George and Fiona McDougall
ISBN: 9780994528506 (paperback)
9780994528513 (hardback)
9780994528520 (ebook)
Subjects: Stress management, Stress (Psychology), Self-actualization (Psychology), Spiritual information
Other Creators/Contributors: McDougall, Fiona, author
Dewey Number: 155.9042

Book design and print management: Pickawoowoo Publishing Group
Front cover image: Kate Adams
Publisher: Siramarti Publications

This book uses paper sourced from sustainable plantations.

Table of Contents

Index of Visualizations and Techniques

PART ONE

OVERVIEW

Work is love made visible. And if you cannot work with love but only with distaste, it is better that you should leave your work and sit at the gate of the temple and take alms of those who work with joy.

Kahlil Gibran

PREFACE

Suzie St George

This book had its conception in a personal journey to Good Work that I began many years ago. It has also grown out of my experiences of helping other people turn frustrating and stressful work into a life-enhancing adventure.

But, above all, it is a treasure chest of the wonderful techniques that my co-author, Fiona McDougall, has shown me. If you are a dedicated reader of self-growth books it is likely that you will already be aware of many of the concepts here; however, it is only by practicing these brain reprogramming visualizations that these concepts can become permanently embodied in how you think, feel and respond to work.

They have great power because they gently relieve emotional, mental and even bodily discomfort while at the same time establishing a steady connection to your spiritual centre. The resulting union between your personality and your spiritual nature allows wisdom and love to flow into every decision you make and every action you take. For this reason, they have the potential to significantly transform your experience, not only of your work but also of your whole life.

All techniques have been tested and refined with committed groups of students over a decade. As a result of putting them into real life contexts, we are now able to describe the processes, both conscious and unconscious, that create Good Work: work that not only puts bread on the table but also supports the growth of you as a whole person, expresses your soul gifts[1], and contributes creatively to a bigger picture.

This, then, is a story written by many people but because its origins rest with me, I absolve Fiona and our students of responsibility for any eccentricity you may perceive in the philosophy expressed here.

Our Story

During the '80s I was a high school English teacher. I loved the job because it drew upon my love for creative language and young people's vitality and potential. But, for a variety of reasons, the work gradually became less and less comfortable until in 1986 I suffered an alarming moment.

I was standing in front of my Year 12 literature class, droning on about a prescribed novel I didn't much like and thought unlikely to have much meaning for 17-year-olds. Suddenly my voice disconnected itself from my body and seemed to be emanating from somewhere outside myself, as if I were a ventriloquist.

I realized that, like 86% of the Australian workers questioned in a 2009 job satisfaction survey[2], I had become disengaged from my work: and that the problem was serious! This was so frightening that as soon as class ended I tendered my resignation.

It wasn't surprising that I had reached this dire state. I was working at teaching related activities seven days a week. I was extremely stressed by a

---

1 We use the concept of soul to refer to the energy that fires the unique essence of a person's life. The soul is a reservoir of unconscious wisdom and the gifts that give direction and shape to the life.

2 Job satisfaction rates vary according to the type of industry and the economic conditions of different countries over time. This statistic is at the very high end of the scale. The usual range of dissatisfaction is around 44-66%.

job that, owing to administrative responsibilities for which I have no natural aptitude, demanded that I be in total control of detail all of the time. I was bordering on chronic fatigue, rarely exercised, and had no friends beyond my work colleagues. My family life was something I prefer not to think about.

My spontaneous decision to resign forced me to consider how I might find a new career. I wanted one I could enjoy as much as my early teaching days, but where I was not subjected to the stress of demands I could not fulfill. You might say that I had begun all those years ago to reflect on what Good Work was, and this, in turn, led me to ask myself why I had got into such a mess.

I soon recognized that I had been on a path that millions of other people were also following: work that was physically and emotionally debilitating. I knew that if I were to get off this self-abusive way of life I must make a firm decision to let go of the perspectives that had led me there. In short, caring for myself had to be the basis for all decisions about my future career.

Later I began to research the history of what I now call humanity's Work-is-Sorrow mindset, and the reasons for its current form. I felt better for the knowledge; at least I now had a rational explanation for my moment of temporary insanity, and a few clues for avoiding it in the future. I did not, however, know how I had allowed myself to reach such a point.

It was not until my retraining as a psychotherapist that I learned that the downhill slide was due to my unconscious acceptance that if work became unpleasant it was to be endured rather than confronted effectively. I could whine about the discomforts and indulge in theories about how 'they' (the school administrators) could improve my lot, but I never had any conviction that the solutions I dreamed of would ever materialize. And, of course, I did not believe I could change the situation without sanctioned support. For this reason, I decided that in my new job I would be self-employed so that I could be in charge.

The step into self-employment definitely gave me better control. I was able to return to my natural talents and organize the workload to suit myself, but it certainly did not diminish my anxieties. The freedom I had achieved was traded for financial instability and exposed me to a different set of inner limitations.

I was not to find solutions to these problems until a decade later I met Fiona McDougall, an intuitive counselor who had studied many forms of healing, and who shared one of my primary interests: how to create a spiritually powerful life. With her guidance and friendship my discovery of Good Work unfolded.

A New Way: A New Life

Early in 2000 Fiona introduced me to her spiritually orientated brain reprogramming techniques. These visualizations, born out of her remarkable capacity to create uniquely powerful inner journeys, profoundly improved my ability to cope with the anxieties of being self-employed. As I became calmer and stronger I regained my former enthusiasm for work. To my great surprise, my newly fashioned career was also far more productive. I could do the same amount of work in half the time with plenty of room for the rest of my life.

It was then that I realized Fiona's techniques had led to the transformation of my own Work-is-Sorrow mindset; instead of unquestioningly accepting work stress as inevitable, my new and creative perspective meant that I was no longer dependent on outside conditions or the goodwill of others to be happy. I had discovered Good Work!

This revelation was incredibly exciting professionally as well as personally. I had a vision of what work that expressed an individual's spiritual gifts without the hassle of the usual limitations could do on a broader scale. I began to imagine how amazingly different the world would be if everyone could love her or his work because it was free of anxieties, drudgery and pressures imposed by external factors.

Owing to our shared interest in human potential and spiritual self-expression, Fiona and I then decided to work together as personal development educators, combining her techniques and guidance with my skills in teaching, coaching and writing. Over time I codified these processes into The Siramarti Personal Growth Process, which we now share with students online as well as in educational workshops.

Here is part of an unsolicited report from one of our students who initially wished to make her work more comfortable, and ended up expanding beyond it. Jane R is an earnest convert to our techniques and her success is impressive. However, without wishing to overstate the case it is, nevertheless, a description of what is possible.

How A Different Mindset Changed My Working Reality: Jane R's Story

'When I was nursing in the late 80's I decided to join an agency to do some extra shifts at different Melbourne hospitals. It was an awful experience. I felt stressed, overwhelmed and out of control and I hated every moment. I did a few more shifts only to find my feelings were identical wherever I went. I never did another agency shift. Over the years I watched from afar as many agency colleagues experienced the same sort of discomfort and stress. Why do it to yourself? I thought.

However, gradually my life needed more work flexibility. I decided to give agency work another go – less work hours for more pay was very attractive, and the flexibility a necessity! Immediately the same feelings of fear, stress and worry overwhelmed me, becoming more intense the closer the first shift got.

However, I knew I had my 'brain change' tools that Suzie and Fiona had given me. I set about using them religiously to dissolve the mounting emotions.

Along came my first shift, overseeing the care of seventy residents at an aged care facility in regional Victoria – very scary when you are the only 'go to' person on duty! I used a daily visualization ritual to create the sense that I could be calm, in charge, relaxed and enjoying myself. The night before my first job, I felt surprisingly okay.

The day came and went! I was stunned to find it was incredibly easy! Everything was a reflection of the qualities I had hoped for. I tried another shift at a different facility and it was the same. Clearing the self-sabotaging story that it was just a fluke, I accepted more shifts in both private and public hospitals, in different wards that required different skills, with different staff, patients and nursing demands.

The amazing thing was that none of the new situations made me feel at all uncomfortable. I felt confident, calm and open to whatever was to come. I (was) able to adapt to new surroundings as if I had been there before ...'

Jane's experience, like my own, details the effect of using brain reprogramming to relieve workplace anxiety, but it is more than this: it is also the story of a person who as a consequence of learning to clear her anxieties was then able to expand her work into a private business as a wellness speaker and educator. Knowing how to let go of her fears led to a job that better suits her unique spirit, which is lively, outgoing, and enjoys presenting information. These qualities now provide a new setting for her compassion, and her work also gives room for sharing her knowledge with others. She has gone beyond simply feeling better to being a stronger and more spiritually aligned person. Her soul and spirit are on board.

The Spiritual Aspect Of Our Approach

People are naturally ambivalent when we use the terms soul and spirit. This is because those terms have different and often controversial meanings. For us they refer to those sources of humanity's unquenchable yearning to expand its horizons in order to bring more of the sacred into the world: more love, truth, peace, compassion, healing, well-being, and appreciation of life's beautiful mysteries. People often aspire to those projects that are infused with the magnificence of these grand aspects of the human spirit.

This urge for spiritual expansion is reflected at the individual level in the desire to evolve throughout life into something more. Its form varies according to the unique nature of each personality but it is especially evident in the ways a person goes about exploring and developing their talents and passions: their spiritual gifts.

While spiritual self-growth is normally regarded as a goal reserved for that minority of human beings who are interested in esoteric philosophies and practices, we believe that discontent with work is actually a sign that the soul nature of that person is not being supported or permitted to express itself.

Unhappy workers usually complain that their work is frustrating, tiring, poorly paid and pressured. But when we ask people what they want, rather than what they object to, they are less likely to say that they want a highly paid job than that they want a job that makes their heart sing or that they wish to feel that it is the work they are 'supposed' to do. They want their work to make a difference or to leave the world a better place.

These longings arise from spiritual motivations rather than worldly ambition or survival needs. People want to love their work, and love others through their work.

But it goes without saying, that if a person is chronically self-doubting, exhausted or resentful, they are unlikely to find or be able to create Good Work. We, therefore, invite our students to use our brain change techniques to dissolve their negativities first. We then encourage them to align their dreams and passions for work with focused action that strengthens their ability to make their job more rewarding on a daily basis.

Why Brain Change Is So Helpful In Creating Good Work

Until recently the urge to evolve beyond one's limitations to better express the love that is natural to a person's spiritual centre has been thwarted by apparently intractable human traits that fight against change. Conservative conditioning, the whisperings of the devil, or just plain cussedness have been variously blamed. However, our own work and the discoveries of neuroscience point to the possibility that these reactionary responses are embedded in neural pathways that can be transformed.

Developing new responses is made possible by embracing two concepts relating to the functioning of the brain and its impact on a person's reality.

The first concept is that how a person feels and thinks in the present directly affects the likelihood of long-term goals being successfully achieved.[3] The fearful and self-doubting individual is far less likely to succeed than the one who is at ease, optimistic and self-believing.

The second principle is that it is now possible to consciously change specific negative reactions through brain change techniques that use visualization to promote positive mental and emotional responses, and even changes in physiology.[4] All techniques that transform a person's consciousness depend on the phenomenon of neuroplasticity, a scientifically identified quality of brain function that has overturned the formerly held position that the brain is a physiologically static organ; in other words, the assumption that a person cannot change their experience of reality

---

3 The effectiveness of the practices of both the Mindfulness movement and Positive Psychology education is based on this principle.

4 Norman Doidge, The Brain That Changes Itself, Scribe 2009

because the brain cannot create new pathways.

Neuroplasticity is now widely recognized as important for healthy development, creativity, learning, memory, and in recovery from brain damage. The ability of a person to independently reprogram her or his neural pathways and to open new ones through both experience and imagination is now credited with some breathtaking improvements in the lives of some people.[5]

Together these two principles mean that if, as Jane's story shows, workers can dissolve chronic feelings of powerlessness, anxiety or self-doubt by using effective neural strategies they can utilize the natural talents they bring to their jobs with greater power.

To be a person capable of living life with a sense of authority and purpose, even in an apparently humble occupation, it is essential to dissolve as many self-imposed limitations as possible. The transformative aspect of this book, therefore, lies in the consciousness-changing strategies published here. The principles of spiritually effective living are gradually made real as each person becomes calmer, clearer, and more respectful of themselves and others. A more spiritually evolved personality emerges to direct one's work.

Although readers may conclude that the Good Work techniques here are versions of the New Age practice of creative visualization, the process of making one's work Good is not about simply 'visualizing' it. Instead, the ability to develop Good Work depends on strengthening every aspect of the self that diminishes one's power to create what one wants.

Relieving anxieties and limited thinking is, however, an essential preparation only. It may be likened to ploughing a field: necessary for a healthy harvest. The seeds of your dreams for working life must then be planted in the heart, fertilized and cared for. In short, you must apply your fresh mindset to materializing your desires through grounded action.

---

5 Norman Doidge, Ibid

You may remain skeptical that brain change can have a significant role to play in turning bad or dull work to good, let alone the capacity to alter personal circumstances. This is not unreasonable. Neuroscience - particularly applications of neuroplasticity to the problems of human consciousness - is still in its infancy. Personal experience of the effects of change via these methods is the only proof currently available. It is also true that none of the techniques will integrate effectively unless the practitioner is truly committed to the particular change that it engenders.

Nevertheless, for those willing to commit to personal growth via brain reprogramming, the effects can be far more lasting than actions that make a particular job more palatable.

Knowing how to express your natural spiritual authority is a surer foundation for expressing your love and truth than self-deprecating compromise, self-righteous objection or passive resistance to the demands placed upon you. Regrettably, those responses to the obstacles that currently face workers, bosses and communities everywhere are the more common ways of dealing with difficulty. However, they are veils to the expression of the uniqueness of the human soul, which is where the true power and authority of each of us lies.

Given commitment to be, as Gandhi put it, 'the change you wish to see in the world' these reactive attitudes need not be yours. Freed of fears and often-unconscious negativities, you can learn how to let your spirit guide you on a practical path to the fulfillment and balanced self-empowerment that Good Work brings.

Fiona and I hope you will enjoy the adventure that this book offers you. You are welcome to contact us at www.thegoodworkbook.com.

Suzie St George
January 2016

HOW TO USE THIS BOOK

There is no such thing as a favourable wind for a man who has no idea where he is going.

Seneca

The Good Work Book explores the general principles that underpin Good Work. It provides a variety of core techniques for reprogramming the brain to relieve common discomforts, and also outlines the key skills necessary to transform your job into Good Work on a daily basis.

The need for Good Work and its characteristics are explored in separate stand-alone topics assigned to each chapter, which you may enjoy for general information purposes. Part Five describes how you can make your daily work Good through developing ten key skills.

However, the book is primarily designed as a manual of basic brain reprogramming techniques that will integrate Good Work principles into the ways you go about any kind of work at any time. Therefore, there is no requirement to read the book from cover to cover to get the most value from it. It is up to you to decide which of these techniques are relevant to your concerns – and then to practice them with precision.

Good Work is a self-directed process that can never be taught through a one-size-fits-all approach. Your path will meander according to your situation and personal preferences. Therefore, please read the next sentence twice!

We strongly recommend that you choose to explore a topic, exercise or visualization at the time it is relevant to your immediate situation.

Although the visualizations dissolve the fears, doubts, frustrations and the inner imbalances that prevent work becoming Good, they do not replace the necessity to act in practical ways to get the work you want; they are simply tools that make the path smoother and less burdened with the stress of negativity and limitations.

Therefore, we provide exercises to help you decide what you want from your work right now, what success will look like in the long term, and which aspects of your working lifestyle you want to maintain or minimize.

How To Use The Inner Work To Best Effect

The following suggestions will assist you to get the most value from the visualizations and techniques.

- Don't skip the visualization at the end of this section! This is a prerequisite for most other techniques. It moves your consciousness into the place in the brain where enlightened choices and insights are easily made. Become familiar with it.
- Take time to use the techniques correctly. Fiona's visualizations have precise effects. Don't be tempted to alter the details. Memorize each visualization carefully. Read them several times slowly, closing your eyes between each step to imagine it. Miming the instructions at your first attempt is also an excellent way to make certain you embody each step correctly.
- Similarly, the exercises that you will work consciously may stretch

your brain in ways you are not used to. Give yourself enough time to do them with focus.

- Use only one visualization per day other than those recommended for daily maintenance. The visualizations seem gentle and simple, but your whole body will take time to catch up with the new neural pathways they establish. Doing too many on any one day will cause overload and make them ineffective. Many beginners find they prefer practicing visualizations only twice a week until they become familiar with them.
- Consider keeping a journal of your progress towards your goals. Some people find that keeping a journal to record their progress is a pleasurable and reassuring way of monitoring improvements and increasing self-awareness.
- Patience: Rome was not built in a day. Although you might earnestly practice the techniques, the physical body, the ego and your unconscious mind all mightily resist change. We wish that this were not so! However, physiological resistance is a significant factor in the speed at which change can occur. If you are over the age of 25, the age at which the brain finishes organizing itself into its adult patterns, the tangible effects of your inner work will take time. Although you may expect to feel a little calmer or refreshed after using a technique, our mature students normally take 9 -12 months to report that their lives have significantly improved in those matters they have focused on. This seems a long time, but remember that this is normal for integrating any learning.
- Learn to use your intuition when selecting material. The following exercise is an excellent way to choose the most appropriate technique. It may seem hit-or-miss, but it is a gentle method of strengthening your trust in your intuition, which, as you will later learn, is an important ability for Good Work. Keep the cards you create for regular use.

TECHNIQUE #1
Choosing The Most Useful Exercise Intuitively

1. Using the Index of Visualizations and Techniques, write the title of each separately on small cards. Divide them into two random but equally divided piles.
2. Bring to mind the work situation that most concerns you.
3. Close your eyes, place your hand over the centre of your chest and imagine surrounding yourself in a warm, relaxing light. Breathe this in until you feel centred.
4. Imagine a wise person is standing next to you. Ask this person, who represents your inner knowing[1], to assist you to select the most useful material.
5. First, run your hand over the two piles to select just one of them spontaneously.
6. Lay the chosen cards out, face down. Close your eyes briefly once again.
7. Open your eyes. Select a card by running your hands over the top of them to sense which one draws you, or, alternatively, notice which card springs visually to your attention. This visualization or technique is the one you need at this time.

---

1 By conjuring up the image of a wise person you are directing your thoughts to that part of your mind that holds unconscious wisdom. We later refer to this intuitive aspect of your intelligence as the higher self. The term does not have a religious connotation because the higher self function is a part of everyone's brain, whether or not a person has religious convictions.

Finally a few words for complete beginners to inner work

- If you are a person who has never experienced any inner work through meditation, prayer or guided imagery, you may be unsure about your first practice of Good Work visualizations. The key requirement is to remain relaxed throughout. Find a quiet, warm space where you won't be interrupted. Sit in a comfortable chair, wrap yourself in a blanket if necessary, and keep the instructions on your lap for easy reference.
- Do not be concerned if you do not 'see' the images within your mind. Pretending or sensing what it would be like if you did see them is enough for the technique to be effective.
- If you are too tense to be able to close your eyes or remember the sequence of instructions, read each step with eyes open, then close your eyes briefly to imagine it before going to the next step. This method will be enough to begin re-training the brain.
- Beginners worry about what they should expect when practicing a new visualization. Each person is different and, as this is so, no experience can be wrong. In most cases, you will feel a subtle increase in relaxation or upliftment. If you do not, it may be because you are trying to do the visualization too quickly or are distracted. An excellent way of preventing these problems is to act the instructions slowly until you are familiar with them. Miming is also useful if you tend to drift off to sleep during the early learning phase.

You are now ready for your first step on the road to Good Work: the practice of a very important visualization.

VISUALIZATION #1
The Inner Garden Of Serenity And Well-Being

To make sure your visualizations are effective it is essential to get into a space in your mind where you feel as relaxed as possible. The Inner Garden Of Serenity And Well-Being is that place. This visualization is a preliminary to all inner change processes.

The unconscious mind understands the symbolic language of mental pictures better than words. When you step into an imagined beautiful garden you are instructing your mind to enter a space where it naturally recalls such spiritually uplifting experiences as safety, love, growth, harmony, wisdom and pleasure. Your inner garden is, therefore, the portal to all brain changes that align your personality self with these qualities. If you are a person who enjoys meditating, this visualization is an excellent preparation for it. We recommend that you develop the routine of using it every day.

1. Find a place where you will be warm and uninterrupted: in bed at night just before going to sleep is a good time for many people.
2. Close your eyes and scan your body, noticing where tension, fatigue or stress exists. Relax each part of the body, starting with the feet and moving upwards. Don't forget to include your hands, jaw and forehead.
3. Now take your attention to your breathing. Allow it to slow a little and become deeper. Let your mind wander to the outside sounds and then back to the breathing.

4. When you feel settled, imagine you are walking along a path to a beautiful, protected space in nature. This can be a place you know, such as a garden you are familiar with, or one you imagine.
5. Take time to recall or imagine the features of this place in detail. Listen to the sounds. Imagine the colors. Smell the fragrance of flowers, leaves, and soil. Feel the air. Pretend it is the season of the year you would like it to be. Choose to bring in special features that would give you joy: fountains, pools, sculptures, favorite animals, or trees with sun-ripened fruit to eat.
6. Find a place to sit or lie down in this inner garden and once again consciously relax your body.
7. Now sense fully how delightful it is to be in this garden. You are free of the world. You are filled with warmth and light and love. You are, for this moment, on the best, most relaxing holiday you have ever been on.
8. Resting in this beautiful, serene place, you imagine gold pieces sparkling on the ground all around you. You are drawn to their gentle shine. They glow like drops of warm sunlight. The gold seems to radiate the comfort of this wondrous place. Take your time to experience it.
9. Feel a desire to touch the gold and hold it. It is yours! Scoop up a handful.
10. Sense the golden glow as it illuminates your hands. Absorb its energy. Take your time.
11. When you are ready, leave the visualization, knowing that this comfort can be recalled at any time.

Reflection

What subtle changes did you notice during or after this technique? Your body may feel a little more comfortable than it did at the start: a little warmer, more relaxed or tingly. If it does not, don't be concerned. It takes time for your brain to understand what it is learning.

Using The Inner Garden Of Serenity And Well-Being In Daily Life

When you wish to quickly recall the comfort and peace of your Inner Garden of Serenity and Well-Being but don't have the space or time to do the entire visualization, close your eyes for a moment. Recall Step 8 in which you hold the warm glow of the radiating gold in your hands. Remember the feelings that the glowing gold brings to you. This will slip you immediately into the comfort of your inner garden.

CHAPTER I

THE NATURE OF GOOD WORK

Everyone has been made for some particular work, and the desire for that work has been put in every heart.

Rumi

Our use of the phrase Good Work needs explanation because we are using it in an unusual way. We are not referring to a particular kind of job, the creation of something of moral worth, or even work of high quality. For us, work is Good when any task engages the whole of you enjoyably: when your mind, your emotions, your physical capacities and your spiritual talents and dreams are aligned with it. Your heart is in it. Good Work is an *experience*.

Do you remember a time when you were doing a job that demanded your full attention and you were in the zone? You enjoyed it because you had a natural aptitude for, or interest in, the activity. You had a desire to express that talent. Maybe you were cooking a special meal for friends, designing an amazing kite for your kids, coaching a team or solving a knotty technical problem. The experience of using your talents pleasurably in the service of something you care about is Good Work.

The challenge of solving problems is also part of its fun. You are learning as you go and, therefore, effort and focus are required. However, unlike work that is driven by pressure and imposed expectations, there is a balance between your energy levels and the job's demands so that stress is minimal.

People respect work that holds these characteristics of love, ease and talent because it has a unique energy attached to it: it feels special. But Good Work is personally satisfying because it shares your love in a comfortable way. Multi-dimensional love is at the very centre of Good Work, and radiates out from it.

While it is certainly true that Good Work is easier to create when you are not harried by workplace constraints or expectations, much paid work can bring the same satisfaction and freedom when you craft it to suit your own needs.[1] However, despite the quiet pleasure that is characteristic of it, Good Work isn't a walk in the park. It will not always feel like play because Good Work challenges you to grow beyond your personal limits.

And, of course, no job is without its dark moments; satisfaction in one's work comes and goes like every other rhythm in life. But even when it is not so easy, even when a job is frustrating and dispiriting, it can revert to Good Work as soon as you find a way to restore some form of ease to it.

Good Work is, therefore, dependent on the ability to relieve discomfort *within* the processes of achieving your goals.

Reflection

Close your eyes for a moment and take a few slow breaths. Let yourself relax and then bring to mind a Good Work moment. It does not matter whether this happened a long time ago or did not occur in paid work. Take

---

1 US scholar, Amy Wrzesniewski introduced the concept of job crafting based on her research into how people adjust their jobs to suit their needs. http://som.yale.edu/amy-wrzesniewski

a moment to remember how you thought, felt and acted during that activity.

Recall your confidence and pleasure. Now imagine the energy of these feelings is in the air around you. Breathe in this energy and absorb it into your body. Your body may begin to feel lighter, more openhearted or stronger.

Good Work As An Expression Of Your True Self

Good Work is an expression, a spiritual flowering, of your true self. Learning about your true self's nature is essential for aligning your job with it.

The true self is the person you are when four parts of your consciousness are operating authentically and calmly in a state of love for self as well as others. The true self is totally distinctive in its style of expression because of the amazing range of powers, preferences and purposes that operate dynamically within these four aspects. These are:

- The problem solving, knowledgeable, and imaginative mental self;
- The body with its particular capacities and limitations;
- The emotional self with its likes, dislikes and its loves;
- The intuitive or higher self, which is the source of creative insight, inner wisdom, psychic experiences and bigger purposes.

When there is a cooperative, balanced interplay of these aspects infused with the energies of love, Good Work naturally unfolds; it is enlightened love-in-action. If a person has no interest in knowing or cultivating the true self, her or his job may provide an adequate income and have social influence, but it can never be Good in the fullest sense.

Good Work As An Everyday Occurrence

Good Work may seem a grand ideal beyond the reach of people who do not consciously aspire to living spiritually. But this is far from the truth. The spiritual nature of a person is regularly revealed in ordinary life: the parent calls upon her knowledge and enjoyment of sports to enrich her children's experience of healthy activities; the man who loves gardening shares tips on growing tomatoes with the next door neighbor; the car aficionado loves helping a friend buy a second hand car.

Good Work is everywhere, but it is rarely consciously invested in as a way to become a spiritually successful and happy person.

Owing to Work-is-Sorrow attitudes the true self is less often recognized in regular employment than in voluntary work. However, this need not be the case. If paid work is to be Good, the more you adjust work to exercise your true self's preferences, the more your income earning can be self-caring and rewarding.

The Making Of Good Work

Balance is key to Good Work. Good Work brings happiness and fulfillment because it balances the need to survive comfortably with the desires of the spirit; you need security and competence to enjoy a job, but your soul also yearns to bring such qualities as freedom of expression, pleasurable connection, personal meaning, and lightheartedness to the projects you undertake.

Most people would consider that good work is defined by its excellence. However, the quality of a service or product alone is not enough for it to qualify as Good Work. There are many people doing their work with a high degree of competence but are worn out or deeply dissatisfied because it deprives them of a good *life*. Good Work, being multi-dimensional in its benefits, offers the best of yourself to others but it also takes close account of the need to care for yourself: to be healthy, happy and at ease even while you are working hard. Good Work loves you too!

The ability to take control of how work is done is often the most difficult of the many aspects of Good Work to achieve. This is not because it is impossible, but because the collective Work-is-Sorrow mindset sees work as a struggle that one cannot change without external factors being favorable. Most people, even those who are highly suited to their occupations, do not even consider that they could make their work more comfortable by letting go of this belief and asserting their right to disengage from the often relentless pressures put upon them.

Good Work, therefore, depends on establishing and maintaining a calm and confident inner environment so that tasks are stimulating but not unduly stressful. When inner peace goes hand-in-hand with your talents and personality preferences, your job will be valuable not only because of your technical competence but because you, as creator, have quiet confidence in it. This self-belief helps you to be resilient to the influence of distracting outer pressures.

This is not to say that there will be no challenge, excitement or change. Good Work is a steady climb that stretches and grows you over time. The effort strengthens self-esteem and helps you to sense your proper place in life. Spiritually, you feel you are achieving 'what you came to do'. At the mundane level it fully supports your human needs.

The Key Features Of Good Work

1. Good Work is not the result of having a particular job. It is the experience that comes in doing any task, paid or unpaid, that utilizes your natural qualities, aptitudes and interests in processes that are comfortable for your own nature.
2. Good Work implies that you have a genuine desire to offer your gifts and personal qualities to others through your job. (Bank robbers and couch potatoes need not apply for Good Work.) Good Work is, therefore, infused with the self-respect that comes from contributing your true self's special forms of love meaningfully.
3. As Good Work is brought into existence by honoring your

individuality in the moment, no one can give you a map to getting to it. It is a journey, not a destination.

4. Good Work supports the whole of you. It does not rob Peter to pay Paul by consuming all your energy, but is respectful of the other aspects of life that matter such as your health, family, and recreational joys.
5. Good Work evolves you as a person.
6. Good Work arises through cultivating ease. The stepping-stones to Good Work are laid down each and every time you relieve yourself of the burdens of stress, doubt, anxiety and ego.
7. Good Work is not static; its expression changes as you grow older, gain more experience and new interests.

VISUALIZATION #2

Reclaiming The Feeling Of Passion For Life

Although it is easy to have a mental appreciation of the characteristics of Good Work, the feelings that Good Work brings are dependent on your brain being able to connect to the qualities of vitality, pleasure, excitement, comfort or beauty that are part of true passion. Unfortunately, as life goes on this ability may become blurred, weakened or forgotten. The visualization below helps to wake your brain up so that you can feel it once again.

The practice is a long one so we recommend that you make a private recording of it using your own voice so that you can relax into it. It should *never* be used by someone else because your voice will alter the way her or his brain responds to the visualization.

The recording will take about 8 - 10 minutes. Mark the points where you will leave intervals to allow yourself plenty of time to imagine the details.

Before you begin, take time to think about your favorite sweet treat whether that is a confectionary, cake, dessert or sweet fruit. Don't hurry this. Be certain that it is a favorite treat.

Make sure you are in a comfortable and warm place where you won't be disturbed. You are now ready to begin.

1. Relax and breathe in and out slowly three times.
2. Imagine now that you are moving into your Garden of Serenity and Well-Being (Visualization #1, How To Use This

Book). Use all your senses to imagine it. Smell the scents, look at the colors, sense the flowers or the water, the animals and birds. Feel your connection to this garden.

3. A path appears in front of you. The path is sprinkled with gold sand. Step onto the path. Kick off your shoes and feel the soft, smooth path beneath your feet.
4. Bend down and take up a handful of the gold sand. Let it sift through your fingers. A shimmer of fine gold dust is left behind, giving your hand a lovely glow.
5. Enjoy the sensations underfoot and colors in the sand for a moment as you walk along this path.
6. Look to the sides of the path. Bring to mind two or three memories of beauty, pleasure, vitality or luscious comfort.
7. Remember the thoughts and feelings that these experiences held for you. You may see visions flickering past as you walk. Let these thoughts and feelings be what they are. Don't judge them for their worth.
8. Stop for a moment. One memory stands out from all the rest. This is a moment of past passion. Let these thoughts and feelings unfold into a picture or scene. This is the one you are going for. This is the one to focus on, and enhance.
9. Take your time. Relax. Breathe. You are doing just fine.
10. Use your imagination to add more beauty, vitality, excitement, or colors to this memory.
11. Move to the side of the path and reach out your hand to the scene in front of you. Imagine you can take a handful of this moment in time. As you bring this handful toward you, it changes into your most favorite sweet treat.

12. Rest for a moment to recall this treat and its mouth-watering scent.
13. Take a taste. Let the divine sweetness and flavor fill your mouth. As you swallow, sense the flavor and texture moving soothingly down through your body.
14. Enjoy the rest of the treat at your leisure. Sit comfortably on the golden sand and remember the feelings of comfort, beauty, vitality, excitement and pleasure that were held within the treat. Let them fill your body and your heart.
15. Rest before coming out of the visualization when you are ready.

CHAPTER 2

THE PROBLEM WITH WORK TODAY

'Oh, you hate your job? Why didn't you say so?
There's a support group for that. It's called EVERYBODY,
and they meet at the bar.'[1]

Drew Carey

To a large extent your working life is a self-fulfilling prophecy. If you subconsciously hold the assumption that you have no power to change difficult conditions your dissatisfaction will continue.

Any belief in personal powerlessness has to dissolve before you can expect significant improvement in how you feel about work. You may change your job, of course, but a fresh set of limitations will soon appear to generate new frustrations and anxiety. Good Work rests in learning how to develop a mind-set that is both realistic and also quietly optimistic in the face of obstacles.

Letting go of negative expectations begins with transforming the psychology you have inherited from past generations. This is not easy to do without reprogramming the brain because the weight of history gives immense strength to such beliefs.

1 http://www.brainyquote.com/quotes/quotes/d/drewcarey389085.html

Throughout the ages very few have been in a position to choose their form of employment, let alone consider the possibility that they could adjust the way they did it to suit their personal needs. The perspective that work is a sorrow from which there are few exits continues to subtly affect most people's orientation to it.

Even people who enjoy what they do are not immune; in fact they may be more susceptible because they tell themselves that the discomforts are a trade-off for their good luck in having a job they love. They downplay the sorrows, but below the surface they are still infected by the expectation that what they have is as good as it gets.

Work-is-Sorrow beliefs, therefore, are like rampant weeds; your own Good Work cannot take root or flourish more beautifully if you do not identify which of them have overtaken you. You must then set about clearing each one from your mind.

Traditional Attitudes

Earning a living through manual labor in pre-industrial times usually meant a life of exhaustion, injury, and often abuse and indignity.[2] The belief that Work-is-Sorrow was borne out every day. Only the governing classes who did not have to use their bodies to eke out a living could avoid the struggle and pain of hard physical toil. Labor was only made palatable by the rationalization that it could in some way lead to a greater good beyond mere subsistence.

With the advent of capitalism in the West a new attitude developed: hard work was promoted as a means to attaining the wealth and status for an entrepreneurial male born outside of the hereditary class. It was also proof of being a good Christian because work was regarded as part-payment on a

2 Only in a few societies, such as Ancient Rome, could slaves aspire to earning their right to become free citizens able to work for themselves.

ticket to Heaven. Whereas once work had been seen solely in survival terms, the newly affluent middle classes of nineteenth and early twentieth century viewed it as serving the individual in a broader way; it had moral credit and social mobility potential, as well as providing food for the family.

For the vast majority of people, however, the larger purpose of work remained the well-being of something or someone outside the self: God or the landlord, the boss or the bank. No wonder that even now only a few – such as artists and craftspeople – see their work as an avenue of spiritual self-expression. Most people in everyday jobs continue to assume that their humble work must inevitably be at variance with the need of the spiritual self to grow and express itself. They believe their spirituality can only be nourished in moments snatched away from toil.

The Modern Employee's Dilemma

Traditional Work-is-Sorrow attitudes are amplified in contemporary work culture by economic skepticism that has abandoned a belief in the practical value of more elevated personal qualities and needs. The spiritual qualities of love, truth, beauty, respect or creative initiative that guarantees greater engagement in work are not high on the list of modern job prerequisites. Even human service occupations are now so controlled by regulation that the capacities for kindly care or compassion are hardly deemed to be relevant to a formal assessment of whether a person is genuinely suited to such professions. As it is impossible to quantify the value of a worker's personal qualities, economic theorists pay little attention to them: much to the detriment of social health and progress.[3]

The banishing of the human spirit from the workplace has also been

3 'Classic economic theory, based as it is on an inadequate theory of human motivation, could be revolutionized by accepting the reality of higher human needs, including the impulse to self-actualization and the love for the highest values.' Abraham Maslow

dramatically exacerbated by modern technology and management methodologies that put the workers and the people they serve at great real and psychological distance from each other. In a smaller world the baker and his customer knew each other, and personal responsibility for the quality of a loaf, good or bad, could not be avoided.

Unfortunately, the organizational arrangements of much of the working world make it very difficult to assert publicly the right to conditions that permit Good Work, let alone create them. We are so hedged in by hierarchies or bureaucratic and legal constrictions that it has become almost illegal to take personal responsibility for making one's work easier or more tailored to individual circumstances.

In short, if you try to change the myriad difficulties that beset workplaces in order to be happier about your job you will walk a very hard road.

However, the personal effect of those obstacles – with the stress, anger and frustration they induce – can be significantly overcome by developing inner responses that minimize vulnerability to emotional overload. Inner peace is the foundation for practical moves to change work because it leads to clarity, better problem solving and more harmonious interactions. Opportunities appear where before there seemed to be none.

Reflection

What negative assumptions about working life did your family of origin hold? For example, did your parents believe that their work was a struggle, undervalued or disrespected? Is that also your experience?

What negative views of your industry or profession do your colleagues or society at large hold?

VISUALIZATION #3
Changing A Mental Belief

This visualization dissolves the negative mental perceptions you share with many others but it does not necessarily change your personal feelings. Nevertheless, clearing commonly held assumptions about work is a vitally important start to Good Work.

Prepare for the visualization by specifying exactly what belief you wish to change, and what you want to change it to. Write out the new belief in a simple but emotionally exciting form that is aligned with the principles of Good Work. For example, you might change 'My work is always being frustrated by others' to 'I can make my own work flow freely and pleasurably at all times.'

As with all techniques you practice for the first time, read the instructions slowly several times before you attempt it with eyes closed.

1. Find a quiet, uninterrupted place to practice the technique.
2. Be seated. Close your eyes. Relax. Transport yourself to The Inner Garden Of Well-Being And Serenity, as described in Visualization #1, How To Use This Book.
3. Invite your higher self to accompany you on this journey, imagining this self as coming to you in the form of warm, clear light that surrounds you in love.
4. Now transport yourself to the top of a dark shaft that drops underground.
5. Step into the darkness and allow yourself to float gently and safely to the bottom, using a parachute if that feels safer.

6. Here you find yourself standing in an enormous old library: your library of beliefs and assumptions.
7. Walk up to the librarian in charge. Explain that you wish to change your chosen negative belief.
8. The librarian will take you to the relevant books that hold this belief. Take the books from the shelf and lay them on a table.
9. Now, on a parchment scroll, hand-write your new and preferred belief carefully and slowly.
10. Place this scroll over the books. Watch them as they magically burst into flame, or begin to glow and dissolve. Allow the flames to consume and transform all the books until a new book appears in the ashes.
11. Take this fresh new book back to the shelves, and then open your eyes gently.

Using The Visualization In Daily Life

The best time to look for a Work-is-Sorrow assumption is when you become aware that you feel powerless in a particular situation. For practice, at the end of one working day reflect on the frustrations you felt that day. Make a note of them. For example, if your boss is inconsiderate, work out the reason why you believe you don't have *the power* to be treated respectfully. For example, 'I don't have the power to speak up for my rights.' This belief is the one to dissolve. Gradually you will find your basic confidence in your power to improve things grows.

CHAPTER 3

SOUL DISCONTENT IN A NEW ECONOMY

Turning and turning in the widening gyre
The falcon cannot hear the falconer;
Things fall apart; the centre cannot hold ...

W B Yeats, *The Second Coming*

Good Work is any act of self-expression in which the powers of both personality and spirit are united in the service of bringing well-being and love to the world, yourself included.

When this union occurs regularly a person's soul is content because human enjoyment is aligned with its desire for a spiritually meaningful life. Difficulties will still occur, but these can be experienced as interesting growth opportunities rather than debilitating struggle.

Regrettably, modern workplaces are, for the most part, highly antagonistic to soul alignment. Soul is considered to be irrelevant to the more important business of guaranteeing financial returns. When push comes to shove, money wins over soul. It does not occur to people fixated on money that supporting the soul nature of workers could actually improve the viability of a business.

This is partly because we have not yet updated a narrow ideology of success that developed during the industrial revolution in which the value of a person's work was increasingly measured in terms of monetary gain. Factory production separated physical work into specialist tasks for greater efficiency and, therefore, profits. Workers became replaceable cogs in production lines designed to produce large quantities of goods needed for expanding populations. Quantity rather than quality became the goal of businesses. The focus, love and rare skills of talented craftspeople fell out of fashion because they could not compete commercially.

At a personal level people began to tell themselves they were successful at work if the monetary return on their effort was good. The hidden costs on quality of life or even quality of service were airbrushed from the overall picture.

The truth that the souls of human beings need more than money to thrive was vividly demonstrated to me during the 1970s when I organized an ethnic cultural festival. Part of that event involved a group of Indian textile workers who were flown to Melbourne to demonstrate their cottage craft skills in fabric printing. They were given the kindest of Australian hospitality, to-die-for pay by Indian standards, and their activities replicated what they did in their village. But within two weeks they were vociferously begging to go home because they had no opportunities to play with their children, gossip with their neighbors, take time out to make meals or practice their religious rituals. No amount of negotiation could quell the rebellion. We had to cancel their contract and send them home.

The fabric printers' specialized work was not intrinsically more stimulating than that of a factory worker or an accountant handling tax assessments. However, because their normal work routines at home had space for the whole of life's pleasures and connections, its tedium was put to one side. Low paid, repetitive work in poor conditions was bearable at home, but the same work, though far better paid, in the environment of an unrelenting modern metropolis became almost instantly intolerable.

I have given this example not to support the notion that we should return to a pre-industrial lifestyle but because the villagers showed me that the usual complaints about poor pay or tedium are not the most important reasons for work being considered bad by those who do it.[1] Rather it is because modern attitudes to work do not support those spiritual needs to love and relate to a real life community that, beyond economic survival, are critical to being at ease with one's livelihood.

Unfortunately, the financial crisis of 2008 has weakened even further an orientation to soul needs. Business has developed an obsession with financial outcomes in order to compete in a diminished global economy. This has meant that employees in large organizations are liable to be assessed as economic widgets rather than human beings with a multitude of personality potentials and emotional qualities. From the perspective of corporations, personalities are messy, unpredictable and irritating in their limitations. Finding ways to control or eliminate personal idiosyncrasies is easier than accommodating them.

For these reasons, employees are generally required to leave part of their humanity out of the job equation, be that emotional, mental, physical or spiritual. But, as soul contentment arises from the joy of whole self engagement in one's work, so that, too, is diminished with often-dire consequences. The fragmentation of the worker's true self leads to the all too well known effects of disengagement: inefficiency, boredom, incompetence, disillusionment and, particularly, irresponsibility.

The effects of avoiding the human soul's desire for authentic human connection through work are camouflaged by the seduction of technology.

---

1 This assumption is supported by studies of job satisfaction in the self-employed. http://www.businessweek.com/smallbiz/content/apr2010/sb2010041_151187.htm

While communication technologies have the power to increase connectivity and knowledge - things we all enjoy - excessive reliance on them is foolhardy: they provide access to useful information but little emotional nourishment. Although there is joy in the power of working with these technologies, for millions the spiritual core of work dissatisfaction is due to the fact that they are discouraged from investing what they do with a sense of caring for or interacting with flesh-and-blood real humans. They want work that touches their hearts as well as expanding their minds. In Australia in 2010 those who were unhappy at work were most likely to be in the industries where authentic emotional interaction was least required such as sales, administration and information technology.

Workers also often want their unique perspectives valued as they contribute to the way work is done. Where work satisfaction in human services jobs is low, it may be due, if a 2012 survey of nurses' job satisfaction can be generalized, to a lack of respect for individual input into management policies and practice.[2]

Unfortunately, despite the soul need for personal involvement, information technology is where employment opportunities are now the strongest. Even jobs in highly skilled occupations are expected to be computerized in the next two decades.[3]

Specialization in the name of task efficiency, similarly, prevents workers from engaging their whole selves in creating the product or service they contribute to. The biscuit designer has no knowledge of baking, but is only concerned with what extra dollars the choice of font on the packaging might bring.[4] At the supermarket checkout, a blank eyed operator's human connection is reduced to a management approved greeting. Her service to

---

2 http://www.buseco.monash.edu.au/mgt/news/documents/nurses-survey.pdf

3 Frey, C.B and Osborne, M.A, The future of employment: How susceptible are jobs to computerization, Oxford University hosted workshop, 2013

4 Alain de Botton, The Pleasures and Sorrows of Work, Hamish Hamilton, 2009

others is so tenuous that when a machine replaces her, customers may feel relieved rather than disturbed.

Vast numbers of workers, especially in urbanized environments, are so removed from the sweat, laughter and tussle of community life that it is no wonder that in discussions about working conditions few see any irony in the phrase work/life balance: life and work are now considered to be mutually exclusive domains.

This probably would not matter if people were, in fact, electronic units programmed to do emotionally insignificant tasks requiring no sense of relationship to themselves or the people they nominally serve. But, in reality, work, though collective in its intention and impact, has a powerful role to play in the development of a unique person who wishes to be spiritually self-empowered through giving love and being valued for that love.

When work is separated from the soul of a person, which is the centre from which health, human progress, creativity, enjoyment and caring spring, the whole world suffers. Things, as Yeats, puts it so trenchantly, fall apart.

Reflection

Does your job give you a sense of human connection to the people your work serves? To what extent does it serve your own emotional welfare in a broader sense than giving you financial security?

If so, give yourself a Good Work tick of approval – or two!

CHAPTER 4

THE TURNING TIDE

Change will not come if we wait for some other person or some other time. We are the ones we've been waiting for. We are the change that we seek.[1]

Barack Obama

Most people want their work to give proof of the value of their existence. This is not surprising because work is a social experience and, consciously or unconsciously, when we work we expect our employers and colleagues to assure us that our contribution is meaningful.[2] If workers do not get this feedback they easily blame others for their dissatisfaction. They look for change outside themselves.

---

1 http://www.nytimes.com/2008/02/05/us/politics/05text-obama.html

2 UK-based Penna, a large human resources company, chose to survey the importance of meaning to employees.
"We asked 1760 UK employees in all sectors and regions what their employers could expect if they invested in creating meaning at work.
55% said they would be more motivated
42% said they would be more loyal
32% said they would have more pride in their organization
22% said they would work harder
20% said they would put in more hours."

However, the assumption that the boss can make work Good for you as an individual is unfounded because, even in the best workplaces, no system or authority can continuously adjust to your individual needs and motivations. In short, you and only you can relieve those immediate conditions that make your job personally unsatisfactory.

This is not to say that employers have never tried to make their workers contented, if for self-interested reasons. In large and depersonalized organizations the need for personal dignity and a sense of positive contribution is often acknowledged by management practices. It has long been proved that happy workers are also productive workers.[3] And discontent can have dire consequences as various workplace scandals have shown.[4]

Management theory also recognizes that human beings love to be given direction that suggests a higher purpose for their efforts. The more inspiring we believe that direction to be, the more we are willing to support a vision that is bigger than our individual selves. For those with particular passions there is a sense of expansiveness to be found in corporations with aspirations to lead the future of mobile media (Apple), or bring inspiration and innovation to every athlete (Nike).

Unfortunately, the mission statement that your workplace comes up with does not necessarily have meaning for you as an individual, and certainly it will not have the power to adjust daily work in ways that suit your own personality's needs.

Current managerial ways to ensure personal involvement in the job are based on models of the past: various hybrids of nineteenth century

---

3 The value of good working conditions and happy management relations have been embedded in management theory since Robert Owen set up his utopian socialist mills at New Lanark in Britain in the late 1880's.

4 Horrors such as the Chinese melamine milk scandal of 2008 or the Bangladesh factory fire in 2012 attest to the vulnerability of communities exposed to work practices that have no heart, no conscience and no willingness to take responsibility for the well-being of all who are affected by them.

socialism[5], Christian work ethic, and twentieth century sports psychology.

The sports coaching model is particularly prevalent in large corporations. Here employees are encouraged to see themselves as members of a team scoring organizational goals. It is assumed that if an employee or manager is coached to achieve her own 'personal best', work will be experienced as meaningful. The plain fare of daily routine with its regular dose of frustrations may also be sugarcoated by motivational pep talks offered by a hyperactive boss or workshops that are intended to focus the mind on the bigger picture: 'Ideals are like the stars: we never reach them, but like the mariners of the sea, we chart our course by them.'[6]

Unfortunately, when such positive exhortations fall on deaf ears, the potential consequences of irresponsibility are managed by putting in so many policies and legal restrictions that few creative solutions to disaffection can see the light of day.

When all else fails businesses resort to pay rises, which they rightly believe will improve job satisfaction rates. The narrowly material orientation to making workers content continues to flourish because people need to eat and will, either unthinkingly or resentfully, compromise their other more complex needs to do so.

Of course, adequate financial return for effort is critical to human dignity - an essential requirement for income earning Good Work - but the spirit-in-human form does not take kindly to having its other needs curtailed by objectives that are solely monetary.

---

5 Robert Owen, A New View of Society or Essays on the Principle of the Formation of the Human Character, and the Application of the Principle to Practice, 1813

6 Cited https://www.goodreads.com/author/quotes/281413.Carl_Schurz

Reflection

To what extent is your choice of job or your willingness to stay in it governed by monetary considerations?

A Revolution In The Making

I have painted a picture of the ingrained nature of our Work-is-Sorrow culture that may appear disheartening. Ironically, however, hope for Good Work is growing as a consequence of the very factors that make it so difficult to achieve. This change is coming about because the various conditions that have imprisoned workers are dissolving. As a result a worker may, with persistence and flexibility, find opportunities for creating Good Work that did not exist a generation ago.

The worldwide financial upheaval that began in 2008 made the Darwinian nature of large organizations particularly brutal; corporate employers often prefer task-specific workers who are psychologically and physically strong enough to weather extremes of stress and pace. However, the effect of these cost cutting and short-term considerations means that the old forms of sticks and carrots that maintained a committed workforce no longer have the power they once had.

Modern workers can find get-out-of-jail cards through retraining, career change, multiple income streams, and new avenues for making a living via the Internet. Bosses can no longer depend on those unquestioned values (and fears) that were once the foundation of workplace cohesion. People of different ages, values and circumstances are slowly starting to take control over the quality of their working life and its outcomes by negotiating their way into conditions that personally suit them. An uncertain, but nevertheless inexorable, revolution is underway.

These developments particularly influence Generation Y workers who view success in a very different way from their parents and grandparents.

Fair monetary reward is important to them, particularly as this sector is vulnerable to the exploitation meted out to innocents. However, personal growth, recognition, influence and work/life balance are much higher priorities for this group than career status or promises of promotion.[7]

In addition, those generations born after the late 70s and mid 90s are not nearly so susceptible to institutional control. Its members, exposed to information previously the domain of a select few, have a sharp eye for double standards, the abuses of authority, and self-serving bias. Skeptical and idealistic by turns, the millennial generations recognize that the world they have inherited has been severely damaged by the blind appetite for unbalanced expansion that underpinned the commercial psychology of the twentieth century.

They are aware that the future is theirs to make alone, and they know it must be different. Therefore, opportunities for self-expressive creativity, entrepreneurial projects, on-the-job learning and teamwork all figure as important factors in their inclination to engage in particular employment opportunities.

Senior workers are also less willing to fit into conventional work structures, if for different reasons. Often seeking extra income to boost their pensions and superannuation, they may be more reliable and accommodating but the effects of aging mean that they cannot work under high-pressure conditions as they once did. Post-war baby boomers require flexible arrangements that respect their physical limitations, but they also expect their leadership, mentoring capacities and social experience to be acknowledged.[8]

Consequently, while chief executive officers may yearn for ambitious, Energizer Bunny workers, and grim-faced managers berate the young for

---

7 Bruce Tulgan, Not Everyone Gets a Trophy: How to Manage Generation Y, John Wiley and Sons Ltd., 2009

8 Patricia Edgar http://www.theage.com.au/comment/government-policy-needs-to-catch-up-with-older-people-20140410-zqswr

their apparent fecklessness, the labor force they will have to rely upon in the near future has priorities beyond the accumulation of money.

These new social attitudes are given extra power and influence as the labor pool in aging populations shrinks. At some point all employers along with government policy makers will need to review their attitudes to individual needs, idiosyncrasies and motivations if industry is to utilize and attract the workers it needs.

Above all, there will also have to be an acknowledgment on the part of both employers and workers alike of the real purposes for which work exists: the multi-dimensional well-being of all who contribute to or are affected by it, including the Earth herself.

Reflection

In an ideal world, what working conditions would suit your personality's needs, preferences and values?

CHAPTER 5

REVIEW: TAKING CHARGE OF YOUR WORKING FUTURE

You cannot escape the responsibility of tomorrow by evading it today.

Abraham Lincoln

It is easy to criticize the system for the dysfunctions and dehumanization of many forms of contemporary work, and therefore the difficulty in creating Good Work. And there certainly is a crying need for a change in the communal consciousness in regard to workplace relationships. The inventing of new ways to work together in equality, dignity and personal as well as collective responsibility is a major - and extremely challenging - task for the new world of the twenty-first century.[1]

However, it is unwise to hold your breath for such advances if you want to make your own work Good right now. Quite apart from the fact that society is always painfully slow to adjust to changed realities, solutions to

1 Signs of emerging new philosophies about work organizational structures are evident in practice driven theories of organizational governance, such as the pioneering social technology known as Holacracy. http://holacracy.org/resources

an uncomfortable working situation in which an individual finds him or herself can never be the responsibility of others.

This statement does not imply that I am dismissing the immense value of past efforts to transform working conditions for ordinary people as irrelevant to making Good Work possible. Neither am I suggesting that we have no right to expect constructive support from those authorities we rely upon for personal as well as professional welfare. Far from it. We ride the same ship of human survival, and the ones who take the rudder have the job, not only of steering the vessel to its destination, but of ensuring that it does not carelessly founder on rocks that endanger the lives of fellow sailors.

However, when it comes to creating your own Good Work where the spirit of individual uniqueness can thrive again in the company of others, we are, in the words of poet William E. Henley, wholly the masters of our fate and the captains of our souls.

The question, of course, is: How can you do this? How can you take charge of your own working life's destiny?

The answer lies in a two-fold process: discovering the nature of your true self – who you really are – as it is expressed in your job, and having the self-confidence to modify processes so that your work can accommodate its needs, powers and also limitations.

This is not easy because of the weight of contemporary attitudes. Your entire approach to your job may require a total re-think. You will need to strengthen your personal power to make work Good.

The Mindset For Taking Charge: A Summary

The following skills and attitudes are essential to make work Good. They are made easier by brain change techniques, but they have to be applied gently and consistently until they become habits of thinking and feeling. The later chapters will guide you on how to do this.

1. Identifying your true self's unique nature, with its powers and limitations, in order to set parameters for work choices and decisions.
2. Commitment to regularly dissolving your personal Work-is-Sorrow beliefs and fears as they show up.
3. Freeing yourself from other people's opinions and expectations about what work is right for you.
4. Willingness to actively dissolve the inner limitations that prevent your work progressing or being powerful.
5. Knowing how to accurately observe, and then flexibly experiment with your work processes to support your immediate needs as well as long-term goals.
6. Making a habit of finding small, pleasurable ways to improve your *experience* of your job.

Reflection

Which of the listed requirements for taking charge of your work experience do you currently have in place?

Which would you most like to develop at this time?

VISUALIZATION #4
Anchoring The Light

The creation of Good Work depends on coming from a place of inner balance. This quick and easy visualization refreshes and balances your energy for the day ahead. It also increases awareness of your real needs and feelings. Sharper self-awareness helps you take charge of the moment, which is the single most important capacity for moving yourself forward. It should be practiced every day.

For your first attempts, stand up to mime the steps to make sure you really are drawing these energies into your body. Once you are comfortable with the instructions, visualizing is sufficient.

1. Begin by relaxing and allowing yourself to draw your attention inwards.
2. Imagine that you are standing in a circle that represents your personal energy field. This is your circle of power.
3. Think for a moment about the things that are good about living life. As you do so, imagine a warm ray of energy flowing upwards from the earth. Let the earth energy flow up the body, and then high above you.
4. Once this energetic flow is established, visualize a warm ray of sunlight flowing down from the Universe, through your crown, down the body to the feet and into the earth.
5. Allow the two rays to mingle inside you.

6. Once you are filled with mingled light, allow it to radiate from the centre of the chest out to the edge of your circle of power. Let it form a cocoon of pure light around you.
7. Complete the visualization by imagining that you put a transparent shield around your cocoon of light to hold it in place and protect it from being contaminated by external disturbing energies.

PART TWO

THE JOURNEY TO GOOD WORK BEGINS

Let your mind start a journey through a strange new world. Leave all thoughts of the world you knew before. Let your soul take you where you long to be...Close your eyes, let your spirit start to soar, and you'll live as you've never lived before.

Erich Fromm

CHAPTER 6

HOLDING TO THE POWER YOUR TRUE SELF

At bottom every man knows well enough that he is a unique being, only once on this earth; and by no extraordinary chance will such a marvellously picturesque piece of diversity in unity as he is, ever be put together a second time.

Friedrich Nietzsche

The starting point, and also the final destination of Good Work, is the expression of your true self. This self is based on your personality strengths, spiritual gifts (natural aptitudes) and the purposes to which you put these things. As well as having all the capacities required to achieve what your soul/spirit dreams for the future, the true self also knows how to make a task comfortable for your human personality. When you are able to exert the power of your true self, Good Work evolves with relative ease.

The true self is the natural character within that knows what suits you. It unreservedly recognizes what is acceptable to it and what is not, not only in work but also in life. It accepts, without apology, that fancy mushroom dishes don't agree with you, it knows that you need 6 hours or 10 hours sleep, it knows what types of information you find interesting, what experiences and people uplift you, and whether or not you prefer a desert landscape to an ocean view. It holds your vitality, needs, powers and quirks. It can never be judged any more than a rose can be judged for not being a tulip – or a horse.

The true self in its uniqueness is the spiritually connected core of your personality from which your special power to create Good Work springs. This self gives a style and flavour to tasks that, though performed by many hundreds of thousands of other people, can never have the same impact. The most valuable contribution you can make to the working world comes from its perspectives.

It is this individuality that has to be honored, listened to moment-by-moment, and steadily nurtured if you are to sculpt your job until it becomes Good Work.

The Difficulty Of Holding To The True Self's Power

Although it is so valuable, it is a challenge to hold to your authenticity. Few people know how to hold to their true selves because they are constantly pulled off balance. If you are fatigued, foggy, or unwilling to look at your real feelings because they might disturb others, it is hard to identify the true self's needs. It becomes easy to give your power away to anyone who is more forceful than you are.

Over the long term you will lose trust in yourself and wonder why nothing ever seems to work out as you had hoped. Self-pity and self-doubt are meals eaten regularly, and you will be vulnerable to any psychological illness that pervades a negative work culture.[1] In short, fear and doubt are archenemies of the true self.

---

1 One example of research on the group effect on individual emotion can be found in Psychology Today, http://www.psychologytoday.com/articles/200307/is-depression-contagious

Unfortunately, the willingness to be aware of what you really want– which always includes the power to create more safety, ease, self-respect, and freedom to express your gifts – usually only comes at the end of a struggle to accommodate oneself to profoundly unsatisfactory situations; the heart, which is the voice of the true self, cries out from the depths of discontent, or even crisis. At that point you will decide that it is essential to make a self-caring change by supporting your real needs.

However, by then you may be highly skeptical that your true self's power is really able to make a difference. The visualization in this chapter helps you to appreciate its subtle capacity to bring about tangible improvement.

The Power Of Personal Energy

The word power is associated with the ability to control or influence people or situations. People whose work is dictated by systems or authority figures usually believe they have little or no power at all. However, when you are able to change working interactions so that others are more willing to listen to or accommodate your needs then you have exerted personal power. Furthermore, you have used this power in the service of the love that Good Work brings.

Contrary to common opinion, the ability to change an interpersonal environment is less dependent on your actions than on the power of the *personal energy* you bring to it. Think of a time when you went to an event where a famous singer was performing. As soon as she walked on the stage the audience sat up and took notice. This was not due to the clothes the singer wore or even that the audience had been waiting impatiently for the gig to begin but because she had charisma: personal magnetism. Such individuals have the capacity to capture their audience with their presence alone. Those who have less conscious control over the way they radiate energy may sing the same song equally well, but never with the same effect.

This ability to radiate energy is not confined to exceptional people. You unconsciously use your personal energy to influence your colleagues, friends, family and pet animals all the time. However, the factor that turns this natural phenomenon into spiritual power is the degree to which you choose to use it to enhance well-being.

The following visualization is a demonstration of how you can improve your physical comfort by intentionally harnessing the power of loving intention to relieve a physical tension or ache within yourself. Later you will learn how to consciously use your energy to protect yourself from the negativity of others, and to bring greater well-being to difficult interpersonal situations.

VISUALIZATION #5
Observing Your Energetic Power

Taking your time to relax is very important for this visualization. Make certain you set up all the conditions necessary for you to completely relax. Find a quiet, warm place to relax where you won't be disturbed.

1. Sit or lie down. Make yourself comfortable. Let your mind drift and rest for a moment.
2. Close your eyes, breathe and consciously relax on each out-breath. Enjoy this moment of relaxation fully. Don't hurry forward.
3. Put the palms of your hands over your lower abdomen. Breathe and relax. Feel the weight of the hands. As you do this you may notice sensations in your lower belly.

4. Bring your attention to the warmth or cool of your hands and notice how this warmth or coolness radiates into, relaxes and soothes the belly.
5. Imagine the warmth or coolness has a color. Play with imagining the color until it is just right for you. Take your time. There is no hurry.
6. You might want to move your hands to another part of your body: a place easy to reach that aches or holds tension.
7. As before let your hands soothe this area, healing the tension. Again you can imagine a color. It may be different to the earlier color. That is just fine. Notice any sensations, then breathe and relax again.
8. Keep flowing your energy and its color into this tension spot until you sense it diminishing or dissolving.
9. Observe how your personal energy has the power to soothe, comfort and heal you. You are not relying on anyone else to make that happen. Congratulate yourself! You have used your personal energy to change a discomfort by using the love that is at the core of your true self.

Reflection

The loving power of your true self is channeled in many ways. It flows through your smile, your touch, your joyful communication of what you know, and in the many ways you make positive interactions with other living things.

Observe your own true self's capacity to influence things for the better by noticing at what points in the day you use such avenues to make your workplace or the job itself more comfortable.

CHAPTER 7

DE-STRESS IN ORDER TO ASSESS

Brain cells create ideas. Stress kills brain cells.
Stress is not a good idea.

Arthur Frederick Saunders

A sad fact of the human condition is that a lot of people like to be miserable. They don't want to change because they would no longer be able to enjoy the drama of whining and blaming others for their misery. Or they believe that battling is the only way to prove how strong and worthy of respect they are. Such people do not wish to reflect on the possibility that life could be different, let alone the idea that they themselves could be masters of their fate. Their case is often beyond repair until they decide they want to be different, and that being so they deserve acceptance and compassion.

However, there is another kind of person who appears to be incapable of change but in fact is not: this is the worker who is under intense stress. A stressed person cannot find Good Work because their internal state is such that if it were to fall like a box of chocolates from the sky they would see it, at best, as something meant for someone else or, at worst, as a mess they have to clear up.

Stress makes the mind inflexible and blinds one to possibilities. It entrenches hopelessness and cynicism. Sufferers are rarely open to hearing that they must assert their right to take charge of their lives. It's a concept that makes no sense in the din of working life.

The paralysis of stress is reflected in a conviction that there is no way out… for a dozen good reasons. It is a form of trance that closes the routes to new places. The very idea of having choice at all seems ridiculous.

Quite apart from a stressed person's closed mindset, the contemporary world often conspires to support this imprisonment. Too often a workplace culture is so demanding that people cannot separate their sense of themselves from it. They have no chance of identifying their true selves' desires upon which choices to create Good Work depend.

This may also be the case for the newly self-employed who discover that running a business entails far more than they bargained for. Overwhelm pulls people away from the centre of their individuality where confidence and insight reside, and therefore the very move that was supposed to give them freedom from stress fails to do so.

Unfortunately, stress becomes so familiar that it is easy to lose awareness of it. Its symptoms become tolerated as 'just the way modern life is.' However, denial is dangerous for your well-being in every way: you can't slow down; you are so wired you can't sleep; you find yourself irritable or paranoid at the slightest provocation. Your overall health slides away without any real commitment to taking charge of it.

The effect on your enjoyment of your job is equally disastrous. Tasks you enjoyed in the past are now approached robotically with as little emotional or mental involvement as possible. And, like the notoriously drunken court official who, instead of recording the proceedings of the court, wrote 'I hate my job, I hate my job, I hate my job' over and over, you could also be in danger of rebelling in ways that will catapult you into the shockingly cold water of the unemployment pool.

Reflection

What ways do you use to de-stress? Which of these do you consider are healthy and genuinely revitalizing? How often do you allow yourself time for these moments for rejuvenation and relaxation?

Learning To Let Go Of Stress

Regrettably, when people are highly stressed they often believe that taking time out for relaxation is a waste of time. It even frightens them because time out from work is a foreign experience. They feel insecure and restless at weekends or holidays, and are seduced into having 'just a quick check of the email.'

This is where the following brain change technique has its value. It instructs your unconscious mind to let go of stress so that you can come back to your centre quickly without taking significant periods of time to do so.

Even if the effects seem short-lived, using this visualization *regularly* allows your brain to de-stress until gradually you become open to finding other ways to take the pressure off.

VISUALIZATION #6
Stress Relief

This is a seemingly simple visualization but it is very powerful. Brain pathways to relieve stress are often weak in people, and in some cases, they have never been used. So please take your time to become accustomed to it, and to fully enjoy its benefits. Let it move you away from the extreme stresses of your work so that you can enjoy the color and pleasure of life once more. For those whose work is in support of others, this visualization helps you to relieve yourself of others' stress. It reduces the need for escapism, alcohol or stress relieving drugs.

Practice it after a stressful day at work and also at any time that you notice you are under pressure. You may find Stage 1 is all that you need; it gives immediate relief.

However, if you wish to return later to the deeper levels of Stage 2, it is important to start at Stage 1 once more. Stage 2 can be modified to address situations that bring on particular forms of stress, for example, going for an interview or performance review.

Stage 1

1. Choose a time and place when you can practice this visualization uninterrupted.
2. Close your eyes and relax. Let yourself walk into your Inner Garden of Serenity and Well-Being (Visualization #1, How To Use This Book). Enjoy this place for a moment or two.

3. Notice that above you there is a big, puffy, silver raincloud. Imagine that *warm* silver light from this cloud begins to flow over you. As it washes down, let it soothe away tension and fill you with nourishing comfort. Keep the flow going.
4. Now sense the silver light moving into the cells of your body and cleansing them. Watch or sense this healing light flowing down to form a warm puddle at your feet.
5. The silver rain gradually eases away. You may like to imagine that you lie down to rest as golden sunlight now shines on you, radiating into your body. This golden light fills your muscles, bones, and cells with its glowing warmth. Feel this warmth as fully as you can.
6. Rest awhile. Let yourself absorb the healing.
7. Leave the visualization at this point if you wish, or move to Stage 2.

Stage 2

1. Refreshed, you stand and make your way over to a special healing area in your garden. Take the time to enjoy creating this place, imagining it in detail.
2. Stand in the healing space. A lighted circle of personal power surrounds you.
3. A good and caring friend appears on the outside of your circle. This person may be a person you know, or one you imagine. They are now going to assist you by pulling out the areas of condensed stress held within your body, mind and emotions.
4. They start to lift and inflate the stress, forming it into different colored balloons. Some colors represent emotions, some

the body, and others the mind. Take your time to imagine this. (When you repeat this visualization you may have more of one color and none of another.)

5. Step back to notice that there is a net or cover over the balloons. This is holding them down so that they cannot float away. Use your will to lift the net. Make this happen!
6. When you have pulled it free, hand the net to your helping friend.
7. Watch the balloons slowly drift away. See them transforming into images that uplift or give you feelings of serenity. They may become colors or sounds that soothe and comfort you. Take your time.
8. Let these lovely feelings drift out into the world where they will provide comfort for yourself and others.
9. Rest here a moment and enjoy.

CHAPTER 8

COMPASS POINTS FOR CHANGE: DREAMS FOR YOUR LIFESTYLE

People here are funny. They work so hard at living, they forget how to live.

Mr. Deeds Goes to Town, 1936

Unfortunately, the sterility of much contemporary work combined with concerns about your present situation means that you probably don't believe that Good Work is a genuine possibility. You may have no idea what Good Work could possibly look like, and our earlier advice that you need to take small steps to get there will seem somewhat ridiculous.

However, you are likely to agree that your occupation, with its pleasures and sorrows, *is* your life for much of the day: and that you sometimes yearn for something more from it. You want to feel that your work is taking you to a better place.

This yearning for something more is the spiritual driver behind all growth in humankind. It is the grand source of our creativity and our love, and without it workers are little more than robots in the flesh. The problem is: In what direction does this 'something more' lie?

Strangely, the compass for finding what you desire in work can often be discovered by identifying what you want for the expansion of your entire life, not just your job. An audit of how and where your life does nourish you, and where it does not, is a helpful starting point for identifying where making changes, including adjustments to your job or job choices, might bring more joy. It provides the data necessary to open to new horizons.

Creating Your Own Compass

The Wheel of Life Balance strategies described in this chapter have proved to be a godsend for those who want to make sure that their work does not deprive them of a life that is enjoyable and healthy. I bless the two executive Women in Business coaches who taught me these exercises way back when I was choosing a new career after teaching. (I wish I could remember their names to acknowledge them here. Anyhow, I send them and the inventor of this technique my eternal gratitude, wherever they are.)

Vitality is critical to enjoying work and doing it well. Because this is so, the Wheel of Life Balance is an indispensable technique because it reveals a clear picture of where you stand on the solid ground of well-being, and where your lifestyle, including your job, is debilitating. It shows you where you are not giving enough attention to important aspects of life that nourish your whole self. From these bearings you can strike out in a new direction in the confident knowledge that change will be beneficial.

TECHNIQUE #2
The Wheel Of Life Balance

Take a moment to study the Wheel of Life diagram. You will see that it divides life into eight sectors that represent the key areas of activity and concern.

By rating your sense of well-being in each of these sectors you can identify and compare the degrees to which you are happy in each of these areas. Its purpose is to throw light upon where you might best pay greater attention to your well-being.

The Wheel Of Life Balance

10
10
10
Daily Management
Mind
Body
10
Finances
0
Relationships
10
Play
Work
Spirit
10
10
10

Although the Wheel is normally used to assess general life balance, in this version you will also use it to assess the balance, or lack of it, that is intrinsic to any job you have or might choose to have. This assessment is essential because every occupation inevitably has limitations as well as benefits. If the limitations of a job create unavoidable imbalance, then it is certainly time to consider ways to redress it.

There is no reason why you cannot add other sectors to the Wheel to suit your situation. For example, many of our clients need to add a sector for Rest, and others who want to evaluate their progress in getting a new project off the ground add an extra sector to keep this aspect to the forefront of their minds.

Don't try to do all the exercises for the Wheel of Life Balance in one sitting. Give yourself time to integrate the insights you gain from each of them. If you complete these investigations over a week or more, it will not be too long.

This is a subjective exercise. Don't be concerned about its objective truth. Tomorrow you may have changed your mind a little in but the overall pattern of ratings will stay the same.

Deciding Your Ratings: Some Recommendations

Spiritual well-being

When assessing the well-being of your spirit, let go of any religious associations with this word. Instead consider how happy you are with your ability to find inner peace, inspiration, insight, self-discovery, or pleasurable self-expression. (These will, of course, be affected by spiritual practices such as meditation or prayer.)

Problematic areas

In some cases you will notice that an extreme situation distorts your ability to give a general rating to a sector. The most common of these are chronic health problems, an immediate financial issue, or a difficult relationship with a person important to you. When this occurs create a new sector for that issue and rate it separately from the general sector. Example: An uncomfortable relationship with your son that rates as 4/10 should be given a separate sector from your generally positive relationships, which you might assess as being 7/10.

Satisfaction with work

When you rate your work, do not assess it on the basis of the income it gives you or the impact of colleagues, but solely on the degree of satisfaction you get from its actual activities. The issues of finances and relationship are evaluated in their separate categories. If your rating is low for work it means you need to consider how you might seek *activities* that are more energizing and growth orientated, either within your current employment or through extra training.

Stage 1: An Overview Of Whole-Of-Life Balance

1. Using a sheet of A4 paper, draw a diagram of The Wheel Of Life Balance as shown, with each sector labeled appropriately.
2. Create a rating scale on each spoke. Write the number 1 at the centre of the Wheel. At the end of each spoke, write 10. A score of 1 (at the centre) will indicate extremely poor well-being and 10 (at the perimeter) exceptionally high.
3. Now give a rating for each sector to indicate your *felt* sense of well-being for each of them. Mark the point along the spoke to indicate the score you are giving it.
4. Note the lowest two ratings. These indicate the sectors that are most calling for attention. If you improve your well-being in those areas, you will increase your energy levels, which will indirectly support your work.
5. Ask yourself what small, easy step could you take to improve just one of these weak areas in the near future?

Stage 2: Applying The Wheel Of Life Assessment To Your Work

Very few jobs can supply whole-of-life support; therefore, in creating the high degree of life energy required for Good Work, it is helpful to reflect on how and where your needs are being met at work and where they are not so that you can make adjustments.

Re-draw the Wheel of life. Now rate how your main work (paid or unpaid) already nourishes your well-being in each of the other sectors. Examples: Your job may give plenty of scope for improving your mind so you give it 8/10 for the Mind sector. If you enjoy the people in your work team, then you might give the Relationship sector 7/10.

Notice which sector/s are the least satisfying. This information pinpoints the areas that need most attention *in your job* in order to move it towards Good Work.

Stage 3: Evaluation

Compare the two diagrams. Do the lowest scores on both Wheels fall in the same sector/s? For example, do you have a low score for general bodily well-being as well as your job? If so, you have urgent work to do! You know where to begin.

Stage 4: Choosing The Point Of Easy Change

You may have more than one low rating, or still don't know where to start. In this case choose the sector that is easiest or most enjoyable to change. An internal change, such as clearing an assumption that you are powerless to improve this limitation (Visualization #3, *Changing A Mental Belief*, Chapter 2) is very effective for weak sectors.

In Summary

Don't kid yourself: work and the rest of your life cannot be separated. The impact of work inevitably affects your lifestyle. The kind of occupation you have chosen (including being a parent) largely determines how much time you must spend at it, what kinds of people and personalities you interact with, what types of life experiences you have, and how much learning, freedom and material security it offers. As a result, your life is inevitably both enriched and restricted.

However, restrictions need be no real problem if you develop a habit of adjusting your tasks to meet your need for greater well-being by committing time to the activities that give your true self the balance it needs. A focus on supporting your well-being in gentle, easy ways is the true north for all Good Work decisions.

CHAPTER 9

MAKING DREAMS REAL

Dreams pass into the reality of action.
From the actions stems the dream again; and
this interdependence produces the highest form of living.
Anais Nin

Good Work comes into existence as the result of using the functions of both hemispheres of the brain to reach your goals[1]: the right brain brings imagination, vision, and unconscious energy to your goals, and the left-brain's ability to problem solve breaks down the vision into small, doable steps to bring a dream into reality. The two functions go hand-in-hand.

The right brain is the home of imaginative creativity. It envisages possibilities and draws spiritual energy from the unconscious to turn your desires

1 The vast majority of people have a preference for using one brain hemisphere's functions over the other when solving problems or handling stress. We define these two types of individuals as right-brain orientated 'Sky' dreamers or left-brain 'Earth' doers. Sky individuals love to dream of possibilities while Earth people love working with people cooperatively in grounded action. Good Work requires that you learn to use both hemisphere's functions in a balanced way. For more on creative balance, see Chapter 18.

into reality. Right brain consciousness inspires, brings intuitive insights and the vitality of one's passions. However, it must be balanced by left-brain practicality that builds competence, and the power to get things done. The grounded actions of the left-brain are the acorns that grow into the mighty forest that the right brain dreams of.

Pragmatic people with a preference for left-brain action often reject the idea that imagination is important in making desires come true. For these folk, dreaming is easily dismissed as New Age airy-fairy escapism or, worse, a sign of impending mental illness. They will point out that success is built on hard work and will trivialize the input of the inspirational right brain.

However, realizing a dream for your working life is more than seeing a possibility and bringing it into form. True self dreams imply the delightful state of wholeness that goes with reaching it. When every aspect of you sees benefit in a dream, the voice of the true self – the heart – can be heard. Therefore, bringing Good Work to fruition is not just dependent on the ability to see possibilities in your mind's eye or to act upon them. It is the ability to *feel* your dream ahead of time as a whole-of-self experience. This embodiment of a dream provides the necessary drive to attain it and also opens you to your higher self's intuitive guidance.

For these reasons, whenever you want significant change in your work, it is worth taking the time to write out your dream for it as a 3D living experience. The example of a powerful life dream that follows provides a model; it is a map to keep you on track despite any detours in getting to your chosen destination. Make sure it remains easily available for quick reference.

Here is an example from one student.

'I have a goal to own a little café in the country. My dream is that this is a place where I can indulge my passions for creating beautiful environments where people feel uplifted. It is a place that people who love beauty come to because it is so aesthetically pleasing – all due to my talent for

designing interiors! I have friends who supply my café with beautiful rustic pottery, simple furniture, a wonderful wood-fired pizza oven. Part of the café opens on to a charming small garden with a fishpond.

I have a couple of staff members who are like friends to me and they enjoy simple cooking as much as I do. Their talents complement my skills. One actually likes bookkeeping! And they are willing to do little extras to make things run smoothly, which is important to me as I love things to be orderly. I like my customers who are appreciative and happy to pay a little more for the excellent service they get.'

You will notice that this example – which could go on much longer – has visual detail, but it also has emotional information and deals with the physical realities of owning a café. It incorporates the spiritual aspect in that she plans to use her known talents, passions and preferred activities. It is obvious that this dream is about ease, creativity and the higher expression of her special talents.

Although it is romantic, logical considerations have not been ignored because she mentions the conditions she will need to make the café run smoothly.

She also wisely mentions her market: people who love to be uplifted by environmental beauty. It is my experience that you should never consider self-employment if you don't ask yourself *what* types of people you want to serve and *why* they will benefit by your work. Your heart becomes connected to your future Good Work through finding detailed answers to these two questions because your true self is interested in valued relationships. A vision for work that is grounded in emotional preference for the people you will serve is far easier to turn into Good Work than one based on models supplied by other people or monetary considerations only.

The example above shows how the description of a dream is quite different from the left-brain business decisions that will later bring it to fruition. These provide the practical framework to build the Good Work you want; however, a dream expresses the *quality* of the life you yearn to live through it. Even if your dream for your working life, or the job itself, is not particularly romantic, you still need to express the emotional qualities you wish to experience in the future because emotions, rather than concepts, are the drivers of all projects that succeed.

You might think that dreams such as a raise in salary or a promotion to a more interesting job are too mundane or smack too much of materialism to be generated from your spiritual needs, but this is not so if your whole self is truly engaged in the dreaming. Sometimes the form your dream takes is a trick of the soul to draw you into an adventure far more complex than you imagined. No project is too small for dreaming.

The more you take the time to train your brain to identify and imagine precisely how the beauty of your dreams will improve your life, the more useful dreams become to you. The vibrations of felt joy are gradually aligned with the deepest parts of your being. All parts of you join in this joy to bring it into being. Your dreams become your soul's dreams.

TECHNIQUE #3
Creating A Powerful Working Life Dream

Step 1: Create a whole self description of your dream

Using the model above, develop a dream for your working life. You may prefer to create a collage or colorful drawing with labels instead of writing. Remember, however, that for the dream to be embodied in the whole self it must:

- Utilize those activities and media that give you pleasure.
- List the practical details of the physical environment or conditions that your body would enjoy.
- Indicate how your mental skills or interests will be happily engaged in this new enterprise.
- Appeal to your emotional preferences for experiences, people and rhythms of work.

Step 2: Slip Your Dream Into The Unconscious Mind

Once you have completed your description, find a pleasant, quiet place to sit where you can enjoy an inner journey that will embed this dream in your unconscious mind. This will help draw spiritual energy to it.

Close your eyes and bring the dream to mind.

Imagine you are walking around in it. Sense this as vividly as you can so that your body can join in through imagined sound, touch, sights and textures. If you wish to change the original vision to be even more delightful, do so.

Pretend the air is filled with the energy of this joy. Place your hand over the centre of your chest. Breathe the joy into the chest and let it flood through you. Let your body feel it fully.

Step 3: Take One Small Step

The next step is to act on this dream in a small, safe way. This may take the form of research, drawing up plans, identifying anxieties to be cleared, or inventing a way to avoid an obvious difficulty.

Common Problems With Creating Life Dreams

You may encounter the following problems with the dreaming exercises.

1. You find the entire exercise overwhelming. You have no idea at all what your dream might be. If this is the case, go to Day 3, A 10-Day Course In Making Daily Work Good, in which you are shown how to work from the present limitations upwards to a better future.
2. Despite the clarity of your dream, you find yourself procrastinating in taking the one small action towards it. Don't be concerned. The reasons for this resistance and the visualization to release it can be found in Chapter 10.

PART THREE

CLEARING THE REASONS WHY NOT

Faced with the choice between changing one's mind and
proving that there is no need to do so,
almost everyone gets busy on the proof.

John Kenneth Galbraith

CHAPTER 10

YOUR FEAR OF CHANGE

We would rather be ruined than changed,
We would rather die in our dread
Than climb the cross of the moment
And let our illusions die.

W. H. Auden

Fear of change is the single most powerful reason for resisting the chance to turn a job into Good Work.

While anyone who genuinely desires a more comfortable working life can create it, this truth is rarely appreciated because, at many levels, people don't want to accept it. They come up with a zillion reasons why not. Fear of change gets in the way of actions that will bring dreams to life.

For this reason it is important to re-read this chapter from time to time, and to practice the visualization at least twice now as well as whenever change is on the horizon.

Any change, whether large or small, is uncomfortable because the unconscious mind, and its trusty servant the brain, prefers physical circumstances to stay predictable and well understood. Even when an anticipated change is welcome, the brain has a physiological reluctance to doing things differently; this resistance stands in the way of fashioning a more self-honoring way of approaching work.

Apart from physiological resistance it is emotionally nerve-racking to open to new potentials. Each of us is aware that change may lead to unintended consequences and, therefore, regrets. What will happen if you ask for your rights at work to be respected? Will you find it impossible to find a new job owing to your age, lack of qualifications, or the state of the economy? How do you know if a change will actually be better? Most people decide that they would rather put up with the devil they know than the devil they don't.

Even the use of brain reprogramming techniques causes anxiety because of an assumption that changing your consciousness will turn you into a different person who will mysteriously abandon your values, goals and responsibilities or, worse, be required to take on more of them! This fear is unfounded. In Good Work, your true self is in charge of *all* your decisions. It cannot take you where you do not want to go.

Of course, resistance is logical because poorly considered leaps into an unknown are risky. However, the methods for creating Good Work do not involve risks that you cannot handle; they never require radical action. Rather the creation of Good Work primarily depends on taking small inner steps to relieve your anxieties internally before you take any action at all. It is crucial to adjust your mind so that it feels more willing and able to make such moves, even if the move you make is as uncontroversial as exercising the right to eat lunch away from your desk. Once doubts and fears are dissolved, the way to safe action often becomes blindingly obvious.

Nevertheless, despite all Good Work arguments to the contrary, most people will put off making choices and decisions until forced to do so by crisis. This is where the following visualization is exceptionally useful. You can use it as general preparation even before you become aware of a need for specific change.

Practice it several times now and then return to it when you are aware that a major shift in circumstances is on the horizon.

The visualization is long and may be difficult to memorize. If reading it slowly several times is insufficient, we recommend you record it in your own voice with a lengthy pause between each step.

Caveat: Do not share this recording with even your nearest and dearest. It will be disappointing to them because your voice will affect the way their brains 'read' it, rendering it ineffective.

VISUALIZATION #7
Releasing Fear Of Change

1. Choose a time when you will not be interrupted for at least 15 - 20 minutes.
2. Close your eyes. Check that you feel warm and comfortable. Remove any discomforts. Make sure your spine is straight, and your legs and arms are uncrossed.
3. Take a minute to let your whole body relax bit by bit. Bring to mind the possibility of changes in your working life, whether large or small.
4. Imagine that you are surrounded in a beautiful green light.
5. Sense that a wise person is sitting with you. Ask this person why you would fear a change in your working life *but do*

not attempt to get an answer. (This question only sets the direction for the visualization to target the part of the mind where such anxieties rest.)

6. You find yourself transported to a comfortable armchair in a large room with high ceilings. Enjoy this for a time. Your body is totally supported.
7. Relax once again. Relax completely. Your mind is becoming as light as a feather.
8. Imagine you are lifting out of the chair. You stretch up, and float slowly upwards. Look up. A large opening appears in the ceiling above you. You see the blue sky through it.
9. Glide through the roof space, feeling comfortable and safe. Now you are floating high above the land below. As you look down you see a new land of strong, vibrant colors: a very solid, abundant land, buzzing with life and health. It is very clear and very enticing.
10. You see a place down there that seems just right for you. You let yourself drift gently downwards to it. Your feet touch the ground.
11. Notice what the ground looks and feels like. Imagine your surroundings. Smell the fragrances. Touch. Listen. Enjoy these new sensations.
12. You now see or sense a color pooling at your feet - a color that is symbolic of the solidity, beauty and abundance of this place. This color, thick as paint, begins to radiate up your legs and gradually fills your whole body. Take your time to feel it. It starts to radiate out from you. Now you are glowing with color.

13. You see a path where you can walk for a short time to enjoy the beauty of this new place.
14. The path leads to a wide, shallow river flowing over white sand. The river is gently moving, and the water is crystal clear.
15. Walk towards the riverbank. Lean forward and cup your hand to hold a little of the clean water, just enough for one sip. It is very refreshing.
16. Now move into the water until it reaches your knees. Sit down to touch the soft, sandy bottom of the river. Gradually submerge your whole body until the water supports you. Then let your head sink as if you have become an underwater creature. You can breathe underwater and you rest there, feeling the clean river water flowing over, around, and finally through you.
17. Recall your work situation for a moment and why you want to alter it. Any unconscious discomfort with this possibility will be registered in sensations of tension or weakness in the body. Let the water wash away your fears that are hidden there. Imagine them as scraps of paper or packets of energy. Consciously choose to let them go.
18. Remember your question: What are your fears of change? Don't be concerned if the answers don't come now. They will slowly reveal themselves over the next day or two if you pay attention to your thoughts and feelings. Even if they do not, do not be concerned. The visualization will have dissolved them to a significant degree.
19. Feeling revitalized, you stand up and slowly make your way to the opposite bank of the river. There is a warm, dry,

soft towel waiting for you. Wrap it round you. Enjoy the warmth of the sun. Watch the river bubbling by.

20. When you feel ready, come slowly back into the waking world.
21. Write down any insights that have come to you during the visualization, including any ideas you have for taking action to ease anxiety about an imminent change. If you cannot think of any practical step, but can now identify the specific anxieties and worries you have, use the visualization, Visualization #15 *The Jell-O Wall: Moving Beyond Anxiety And Worry*, Day 1, A 10-Day Course In Making Daily Work Good, to clear them one by one.

Releasing Fear Of Change puts you into a mental space where you will be open to the idea of taking charge of new directions, large or small. However, remember that inner work often has to be followed by actions that will lead you forward.

Here is an example from Kate A who acted on her desires after clearing her fears of negotiating her boss's plan to change her job. It is obvious from her report that as an employee she was highly valued because she was competent as well as being a cooperative person to work with. However, she was not at the time confident with negotiating work changes. It was Kate's newfound ability to let go of her internal fears that made her able to do so with such resounding success.

'Hi Suzie,

I just wanted to share my day with you, after our session last week (on clearing my fear of asking for a change in work conditions).

It turned out my boss was away on Friday, so we didn't get to have our meeting about my long-term employment conditions as we'd planned.

Then on the weekend, I kept coming across two very distinct types of people - people who gave away their power ('Well, that's just the way the world works' types) and people who did sensational things because they followed their hearts. These examples were strangely obvious.

I watched my emotions carefully and I found the people who gave away their power stirred anger and repulsion in me, and the people who followed their hearts became instantly inspiring and made me spark with energy. I made a decision that I would be one of the latter - it may be scary at first to make a decision that followed my gut, but that wouldn't compare to the discomfort I'd feel long-term if I went against my true feelings.

So today I had my meeting with my boss (after doing some visualizations to help me clear my anxieties and set the right energy for the discussion). My boss started talking about these wonderful jobs he wanted me to head. I expressed my gratitude, then told him that I wanted to only work 4 days, not 5. I was honest, saying that I'd worked hard to achieve a work/life balance, and wanted to retain that so I could be of value to the workplace, and myself.

He said that my energy was something they valued, and understood my needs. Then he offered me permanent work of four days a week, changed my job description to include creative projects, and offered me paid holiday/sick leave!

If I ever wanted proof that it pays to look after yourself, that was it!'

CHAPTER 11

BANISHING THE VOICES OF THE PAST

There is no such thing as a good influence. Because to influence a person is to give him one's own soul. He does not think his natural thoughts, or burn with his natural passions... He becomes an echo of someone else's music, an actor of a part that has not been written for him.

Oscar Wilde

The process of discovering Good Work can usefully begin with banishing those past influences that distract you from knowing how you, as a unique individual, operate.

The most potent source of an inability to let your true self guide your work choices and decisions is likely to be your family of origin. Your family's attitudes permeate the air that your unconscious mind breathes; the working lives of parents, and their attitudes about the challenges of earning a living are the only model of the working world that young children know.

Good parents give great gifts of love and a heritage of expertise in their fields of endeavor that can strengthen a person's self-esteem and confidence.[1] However, they are unwittingly often the source of a person's inability to recognize her or his uniqueness. Our parents' perceptions of what is acceptable work, their own disappointments and ambitions, their worries and their teachings profoundly affect the unconscious limitations we put upon ourselves, even though such concerns are not necessarily relevant to the true self.

This is illustrated in the following case.

A woman in her late thirties came to me for counseling. She was extremely distressed, confused and directionless. She wanted help because she was experiencing persistent and overwhelming fatigue. As we talked it became clear that she was overworking, and that there was no obvious reason why she was putting in so much effort.

I asked her to observe her daily activities, and each time she moved into a new task, to ask herself the question, 'Who says I have to do this?'

The effect was dramatic. She returned with a list of observations many pages long and a single statement that read, 'I do most of this because my mother – who I do love – believes this is the way to lead life.'

Then she added, 'There is no real need for me to have this consultation with you because virtually none of this is me. I know what I have to do. I have got to stop this.'

I saw her once again several months later. She was a transformed personality: vibrant and calmly assertive.

This is a vivid example of where a person did not know who she was

---

1 According to research conducted by Nielsen, 'fathers generally have as much or more influence than mothers on many aspects of their daughters' lives. For example, the father has the greater impact on the daughter's ability to trust, enjoy and relate well to the males in her life... well-fathered daughters are usually more self-confident, more self-reliant, and more successful in school and in their careers than poorly-fathered daughters ...' (2007, p12). Following this research, a US study of college undergraduates indicated that a father does have influence over his daughter in many areas, including body image and sexuality. http://www.kon.org/urc/

because she had, as a child, absorbed mother's teachings and expectations, and had never questioned them. Because she loved her mother, she had continued running her life her mother's way well into adult life.

This problem often extends to a choice of jobs. Many people have jobs that are not reflective of their true selves because the beliefs, experiences and unspoken prejudices of their parents blind them to other possibilities.

This compliance later extends to peer relationships when men avoid reconfiguring their working lives to suit themselves for fear of the disapproval of other men, or when women are consumed by anxieties as they try to fit themselves to peer group's theories of appropriate womanhood. These people are afraid of doing things differently. Yet Good Work is always different because it is an expression of spiritual individuality.

Reflection

Draw to mind your current occupation/s, whether in paid employment or unpaid domestic, community work or study. Now ask yourself the following questions.

Did your parents' opinions, ambitions for you, or experiences influence your choice to follow that kind of work?

Do you want success in your work/study to prove yourself to one or both of your parents?

What difficulties in work/study did your parents experience? Examples: They were underpaid, worked overly long hours, had a job that entailed a high degree of responsibility, were often unemployed, or had failed ambitions to follow a particular career. Are you repeating that history?

VISUALIZATION #8
Banishing The Voices Of The Past

Once you have completed the reflection exercises, you are ready to do this visualization. You will need to be completely familiar with Visualization #1, *The Inner Garden Of Serenity And Well-Being,* How To Use This Book, and Visualization #4, *Anchoring The Light*, Chapter 5. As for all these inner journeys, you may prefer to create a recording of the technique for your personal use only.

1. Find a quiet, warm place to sit. Make sure your back is supported and your arms and hands are uncrossed.
2. Relax and take your attention to your body. Breathe with the intention of relaxing the body tensions on each out-breath until you are at ease.
3. Imagine you are walking the path to your Garden of Serenity and Well-Being.
4. Take your time to sense its comfort, protection and beauty. Bring all your senses to this step: sight, smell, hearing and also your emotional connection to it.
5. Now create a circle of personal power in the grass around you. *Anchor The Light* through this circle as described in Visualization #4, Chapter 5.
6. Once you are satisfied that you have surrounded yourself in the light of balanced energy, imagine a second circle of light at least two metres away from your own.

7. Bring all your family members, even grandparents and great-grandparents, to stand in this second circle. Sense them carrying all their perceptions about work. You might even like to pretend they are holding tight to bags, brief cases, toolboxes or documents that hold these beliefs, experiences, and opinions.
8. Look down at yourself. Imagine that there are cords of energy that flow from you to your family's circle. These cords hold your connection to your family's Work-is-Sorrow attitudes and their prejudices.
9. In your mind, firmly state your intention to let go of any of your family's perspectives that are not aligned with your true self. *Feel your commitment to this intention.*
10. Breathe in and pull back the cords that represent your own attitudes from your family members.
11. On the out-breath release all the cords that represent your family's attitudes, sending them kindly back to your family. Keep doing this for several breaths.
12. Notice that some cords do not release. These represent deeper discordant connections between you and your family, and their desire to have you continue to hold their beliefs.
13. Using the breath, firmly push these remaining cords back into their circle until you feel that this connection has been totally dissolved.
14. Now, look down into your chest. In the centre there is a glowing sun of mingled love and light. Imagine drawing some of this energy forward into a colored ball of love to give to your family.
15. Throw the ball into your family's circle. Imagine that each of them is absorbing this energy to be used for their own well-being.

Further Applications

Once you have practiced *Banishing The Voices Of the Past* for your family, you can use the visualization for groups that you think influenced your decisions earlier in your life: your school, teachers, peer group, or experiences of early work that were negative.

CHAPTER 12

MISUNDERSTANDING THE NATURE OF SUCCESS

You have brains in your head. You have feet in your shoes.
You can steer yourself in any direction you choose.
You're on your own, and you know what you know.
And you are the guy who'll decide where to go.[1]

Dr. Seuss

One reason why you might be hesitant to believe in the possibility of Good Work is a misunderstanding about the nature of success. This is the belief that success is a state of high achievement that is measured by criteria that are visible and respected by others. While external validation of one's work is necessary feedback, the true self has internal measures of success that are equally important because they are the ones that bring the most long-lasting sense of fulfillment.

Most initial choices about employment are based on where we believe we have the capacity to be valued by others, as well as making a living.

---

1 Cited http://www.goodreads.com/quotes/22842-you-have-brains-in-your-head-you-have-feet-in

Young people want to gain a rightful place in society through having their work acknowledged. This is all well and good. But, unfortunately, beyond this point few people consciously consider what personal success at work actually is: what it looks like or how they will feel about it in everyday reality. They think of success as a relatively distant destination that, when reached, will result in public acclaim and reward.

However, for the true self success is much more personal, more immediate and often far less socially recognized, as in the case of an elderly man I met some years ago at a black tie cocktail party.

He and his wife told me that they had been in a car accident in which he had broken both legs. The knitting of the bones took some time so that the muscles atrophied to the point that he found it difficult to walk. Physiotherapy helped him walk more easily but this outcome was not enough: he wanted to feel really strong again.

To my great surprise, he then dropped into a squat and rose confidently, cocktail still in hand, to show me that he had achieved his goal.

'I succeeded,' he said with a boyish grin, as he repeated his squats several times.

His wife, however, looked embarrassed at what she clearly thought was an inappropriately public display of proof!

This incident illustrates a key principle about personal success: success for the true self is not necessarily a grand display of competence or something that someone else will automatically acknowledge or even approve of. It is the achievement of a dream or goal that you, from a current point in life, truly want. Certainly you may have a long-term project in mind that others will also value, but the real joy of success comes through making each step along the way a reason for celebration because it has meaning for you alone.

Many people fail to identify the processes of their own Good Work because of this misunderstanding. They set the benchmarks for success on achieving grandiose outcomes set by others: their parents, partners, bosses or enthusiastic teachers. They do not stop to ask themselves if those ambitions arise from the true self's interests and needs.

In fact, only a minority of people authentically aspires to the extreme forms of worldly success that are so beloved by society. The emphasis on high professional status and exceptional wealth, along with the media-driven rise of twentieth century celebrity culture, results in unrealistic, not to say bizarre, expectations. These imply that to be successful you should be rich, famous, good-looking, prodigiously talented, under-35, and – as one of our students humorously added – *also* be married, have three perfect children and a mortgage. These goals are not defined by your unique spirit's powers and preferences but by society's fantastical curriculum. Regrettably, too many people judge their success by its report card.

Of course, it is absolutely true that outstanding achievements are inspirational for everyone, but the desire for these experiences are only powerful motivators when the essence of them accords with core characteristics of the true self. If, however, ambitions are not the authentic visions of the true self, a working life driven by the pressures inflicted in the name of achieving so-called success can easily become a real misery.[2]

Even those who consider spiritually orientated success to be more real than the worldly variety are not immune to these illusions. In my experience, they often feel guilty for not being perfect examples of the teachings of Christ, the Buddha, the Prophet or their personal guru.

If you carry the pernicious illusion that success means Being Great, you are likely to find it impossible to acknowledge or take pride in the authentic

2 A must-read account of how externally defined success does not necessarily lead to personal fulfillment or happiness can be found in Andre Agassi's autobiography, *Open*, Knopf, 2009

achievements and pleasures of your daily journey. You will never really find your own uniquely expressed version of Good Work.

Here is a reflection from Jane K that makes this point eloquently.

'I have recently been in the fortunate position to allow myself several months off work, a time to reflect, regroup and reimagine the next steps on my path. The first rule I set myself for this time was that there would be no rules. I gave myself permission to let go of all the obligations large and small that I allow to fill my life. I wanted to explore what would happen if I gave myself a clean slate to explore what is truly nourishing from moment to moment, for my whole self.

I think I had a vague idea that my grand life, this elusive, satisfying real life would emerge from this space and in a way I was right, only what emerged didn't look anything like the grander life I thought I wanted.

Instead of using the time to write that bestseller or start a new consultancy, I found myself lying in a pool of sunlight on my bed with the cat, simply enjoying the warmth of the sun and her companionship. I delighted in the emergence of spring and the blossoms on my walk. I enjoyed gazing out the kitchen window and washing the dishes whilst listening to the radio. Most of all I have loved playing. I've been playing with fabric, playing with ideas, playing at house building, playing with design. In short rather than being productive and busy I've meandered, pottered and delighted in the everyday.

The emergence of this happy life, buried somehow by the busyness and seriousness that usually clouds my life has come as a bit of a surprise. I know that I have been yearning for simplicity and yet somehow I feel like I've been distracted from enjoying it by this nagging sense that somehow I have to prove myself in the outer world and do something 'significant' with my life. I've been aspiring to a set of values that are not my own idea of success.

As my time of retreat comes to a close I am imagining what my life would look like if work and play converged. More importantly I'm trying to reimagine my working life without the ubiquitous overlays of obligation and productivity, outcomes and achievement. I'm wondering what it would be like to dance through each day and somehow make a living from doing so. It seems like an impossible dream at this moment, but then again isn't that part of the fun of having a dream in the first place?'

Jane K's experience showed that Good Work for her involves feeling pleasure in the sensory environment. She also learned that 'socially significant' work did not mean it would be necessarily good for her.

In summary, you and you alone know what feels like success in each moment. In the broader picture, feedback from others will, of course, be part of your wider assessment because you work for others' welfare as well as your own. However, a balance between the self and others' needs is the key to authentic success.

Reflection

On a sheet of A4 paper, draw up a Success Pie Chart to represent your attitude to your work in general. Divide it into sectors whose size reflects the degree to which you measure success by each of the following factors: general public recognition of your efforts, (e.g., 2%); the praise of colleagues, (15%); the response of your boss (20%); positive feedback from clients or customers (30%); the approval of a partner or other family members (3%); the amount of money you earn to support your preferred lifestyle (10%); your own assessment of the quality of your achievement (20%);

your satisfaction with how well you managed the processes in getting to the outcome (0%). Totals = 100%.

Once you have completed the chart, decide whether you are happy with the balance between self-approval versus the approval of others. In the hypothetical example given, the balance is 30:70: 30% being self-orientated success and 70% being success measured by the approval of others. Note: There is no 'right' balance here; this is a self-awareness exercise only. It is up to you to make of it what you will.

CHAPTER 13

FAILURE TO SEE THE FUTURE WITHIN THE PRESENT

The power for creating a better future is contained in the present moment: you create a good future by creating a good present.[1]

Eckhart Tolle

Good Work is an adventure into new lands. It is exciting and rewarding because it helps you be in charge of the future. However, failure to observe the realities of the present is a serious obstacle to that future because it is only in the immediate moment that you can make a task more pleasurable or free flowing.

Effective observation of the present is not lop-sided. It identifies what delights you about your current experience and also what frustrates, tires or depresses you. These observations should also be put into the bigger context of where you would like your working life to go. From there, you can decide, metaphorically speaking, whether you are on track to your dreams,

---

1 Eckhart Tolle. (n.d.) http://www.brainyquote.com/quotes/quotes/e/eckharttol571602.html

what new territory you want to explore, what hills you want to climb, and when it is time to rest.

Celebrating your successes is extremely important, too. It stops the brain from going down the well-worn paths of self-criticism or hopelessness. You need that guitar for campfire songs, and possibly a travel diary to record your discoveries.

These habits of observation and reflection become the basis for reviewing your progress; you may find the route you originally chose is too rocky or you come upon a new vista that excites you more. Adjustment will always be required because the road to Good Work is a wandering one; it is not a career ladder.

The reviewing-and-adjusting process often begins as a reaction to discomfort but its real power is revealed when it becomes a proactive life skill. This skill depends on the following capacities:

Developing self-awareness in the moment

The skill of reviewing-and-adjusting is learned slowly. It starts by experimenting with what small adjustments could improve your felt experience of your work. However, while most people can think up logical ways to improve inefficient procedures, few are able to *feel* if a process suits them. A change of focus from the mechanics of a particular task to the *experience* of it requires expanded self-awareness. This is usually difficult because the brain filters out information that does not fit a previously learned pattern. Therefore, you must learn the skill of noticing what is happening to the whole of you *as you work*: when your body asks for a stretch, when your mind requires a change of focus, or when you require some emotional nourishment in the form of a chat with a reassuring colleague.

Reflection

Take your awareness away from reading to your body. What adjustments would make it feel more comfortable right now?

Acknowledging the good as well as defining the lack

Good Work is joyful in a steady, non-spectacular way. Pointers to it can be found in anything that you like – and, through reverse, what you dislike – about *any* working situation: the jobs you do at home, your recreational activities, as well as your preferences for environmental conditions, such as working hours, noise levels, solitude or teamwork.

These details help to map your working style. The more you know these, the easier it is to decide what conditions you want to maintain or promote, as well as those that should be reduced or eliminated.

Small improvements will not, of course, make a big difference to a wholly wretched situation. Having made as many alterations as practicable you may find that alternative employment is the only option. However, when you do choose a new direction, the choice will not be based on a desperate need to escape at any price but on a clear picture of what working conditions maximize your sense of well-being.

Focusing on taking one exact step

Good Work cannot be created upon the instant. It develops slowly as you experiment to find out exactly what works for you, and why.

Imagine that an exhausted office manager notices that if he takes a walk in the park at lunchtime it relieves his stress. This observation points towards something that will be important for him in developing Good Work: a working lifestyle that allows for respite from the pressures of the job. He can choose to make a short walk part of his daily routine, or he can look for a job where time out to do his own thing will be acceptable.

However, knowing exactly how a change makes a difference to your well-being is also important. Not all stress-relieving walks have the same effect. The lunchtime walk will have different benefits for different personalities. One person may realize she needs more physical refreshment in her Good Work life. Another finds he needs a job with opportunities to get relief from emotional pressures.

By identifying the exact nature of the comfort or relief that small modifications bring, you create or look for similar conditions elsewhere.

Knowing how to update your work as you age

At intervals you will need to scan your entire working lifestyle to see if it is still aligned with the developmental changes that occur over a lifetime.

I take my own case as an illustration of enjoyable work gradually becoming less than Good. In the late 1980s when I taught at high school, I would have claimed that my work was, on the whole, a rewarding experience. I enjoyed teaching, my students achieved good results, and my colleagues respected my competence. I was exercising some of my true self strengths for communicating ideas, and helping my students to think with clarity; my spirit was in the work, and the money I made was enough for the family coffers.

The fact that I was teetering on chronic fatigue, or that my relationships were strained to breaking point, was from my perspective just symptoms of the inevitable consequence of a 7 a.m. to 11 p.m. job that had to be 'managed.' It did not occur to me that the reasons that other parts of my life weren't satisfactory were due to my changing perspective about the work itself.

A change had been brewing in me for some time; I had mastered the art of teaching at the coalface and was ready to take a wider view. I became frustrated that my colleagues were disinclined to see education as needing to embrace processes that were appropriate to the students' immediate emotional interests as well as the necessity to be educated in their intellectual heritage. I wanted the power to make my (then radical) vision of more holistic education real.

The school, to its credit, gave me the opportunity to develop pastoral care arrangements for senior students. But my new role involved a supervisory function, which is definitely not a forte of mine. Because I had strayed from my core talents, I grew exhausted, stressed to screaming point, and found myself increasingly sickened by a sense of powerlessness as fellow teachers were unable to support my ideals, not through any lack of goodwill but because they lacked the skills to do so. Such joy as my job formerly held had vanished along with my motivation to make a difference to educational culture.

It is common for people in similar situations to want to down tools and seek any kind of new employment that will relieve them of the discomforts of outdated work. However, they often do it without any further consideration other than whether the new job will pay enough and whether they have the skills to attract a prospective employer.

Fortunately for me, I had long service leave due to me, and this gave me the time for a broader appraisal of my situation.

The act of consciously reviewing your whole working life in order to take a new direction is what I call setting up base camp. It is not, as you will discover, a clinical mental exercise but incorporates felt, and often unexpectedly pleasing, acknowledgment of your gifts and powers.

TECHNIQUE #4
Base Camp Review

This technique is a template for setting up a balanced 'base camp' assessment of any current form of work, including part-time, domestic or voluntary work.

The Base Camp Review is not something done well when you are under pressure or feeling somewhat desperate. Find a time when you can fully focus on yourself: most people prefer a long weekend or a holiday away from the usual demands. Don't attempt all of them at one sitting but break them down into convenient time slots of about 10 - 15 minutes taken over several days.

If you are unfamiliar with visualizing, do not be concerned if your first attempt at this exercise is awkward. You are expanding your brain pathways and, like any new exercise in the gym, you may find it an effort. Just doing the best you can will be beneficial.

Stage 1: Setting The Scene

Step 1

Write down all the main facts of your current employment situation. *Do not make any emotional remarks or mental reflections about these facts.* These are the realities that any outsider or CCTV camera could record.

Example: I work in an office, doing administrative tasks. I mostly work at a computer but I also attend meetings with my boss's clients that get me out of the office. I work four days a week. It takes me an hour to get to work by car. I have an arrangement with my boss to have my annual leave taken in slots of two weeks that coincide with school holidays. My salary is base level and does not allow me to have holidays away from home or money for much recreational leisure. I have little personal interaction with other staff.

Step 2

1. Close your eyes to visualize. Relax with a few slow breaths. Take your mind to a scene that represents your common experience of your job.
2. Now imagine that this working situation is symbolized by a piece of music, a single sound, a color or a texture. Take your time to do this. Let it slowly come to you.
3. Does that music, sound, color or texture appeal to you? If so, why? What pleasant qualities do you associate with that symbol?
4. If the symbol is unappealing in some way, how is it so? For example, it is too noisy, it is harsh in texture, feels cold, or it shows up as a bland or repellent color.
5. Now identify what the unsatisfactory aspect of the symbol actually signifies. For example, if you imagine your job or workplace to be a loud, discordant sound it could mean that you need a more physically quiet environment or, alternatively, that you have too many demands upon you. The symbol is yours to interpret. Keep your eyes closed and your attention on your chest as you take your time to explore its exact meaning.

Stage 2: Balanced Observation

Even if you sense that your experience of work is significantly negative, you require a balanced perspective before you can change direction. This stage helps to establish this balance. If you find that any of the steps are difficult, take time out to reflect on what that means about a need for change *within yourself.*

1. Identify a minimum of three things you appreciate about this situation. Examples: I enjoy the four-day a week arrangement. I like meeting different people outside the office and hearing negotiations. I like having some school holidays off work. If you make a change you may still want these features in your new employment.
2. Identify three skills or personality traits that make you competent in that job. Examples: I am good at simplifying organizational matters. I like to be meticulous. I have patience with my boss whose orders are sometimes confusing.
3. Sit back. Relax. Close your eyes and take a moment to honor what you have achieved at work, however small or large that is. Maybe someone has thanked you for your help or you have observed for yourself a positive effect of your personality in a socially difficult situation. Let these experiences flow into your mind. Notice how your body responds.
4. Place your hand over the centre of your chest. Look down into it. Now imagine these skills and strengths are a light within your heart like a candle flame. What color is that light? How bright is it? Visualize it glowing in the workplace, or to those you work with. How far does it radiate? What is its effect? Are you happy with the light as it is?

Stage 3: Sensing The Change You Need

Still with your eyes closed and your focus on your chest, imagine that the candle flame in your heart is shining on the symbol of work (positive or negative) that you imagined in Stage 1. Watch the effect of the flame on your symbol. Take your time to sense this.

Ask yourself what, if anything, you need to do to create a positive change so that your light will shine more beautifully on your work. Examples: You might realize that you must gain confidence in speaking up more, or give more time to socializing with your workmates. Alternatively, you may understand that your light cannot significantly change the situation for the better; it is time to move on.

Stage 4: Action

At this point you may realize that you don't really need a major change in your work; you just need to improve an aspect of it. If, however, you sense that a complete change is required, you need to act. (You may benefit by reading those chapters in Part 4 that resonate with you.)

The Base Camp exercise will show you both the light and the dark of your current situation. It will also help you sense what is truly important to change right now. Don't be concerned about any 'Yes, but …' thoughts that come to mind after the Base Camp analysis. You may well find an answer to them in the following chapters.

CHAPTER 14

REVIEW: LIFE WITHOUT YOUR DEMONS

I was always looking outside myself for strength and confidence, but it comes from within. It is there all the time.

Anna Freud

Good Work depends on confidence in the power of your natural strengths. But if you have chosen to read this chapter, it is likely that inadequacies and limitations rather than strengths are to the forefront of your mind.

Whatever external problems you face, the most depressing limitations are those that arise from your inner demons: the self-doubt, anxieties, confusion, worry and emotional weariness. These are veils that camouflage your true self's power so that your self-confidence is weakened.

They are also debilitating of Good Work because they muddy the windscreen; it's difficult to see where you are going. And the more that negativities plague you, the more you are in danger of letting other people determine your working life. For these reasons it is revitalizing to sense the person you will be when you have vanquished these demons.

The following uplifting visualization will counteract the energetic effect of feeling inadequate or overwhelmed because it shows you what your future life could be. *Sensing The Future You* helps to inject the energies of hope and optimism at times you need them.

It is possible that you will resist practicing this visualization. Paradoxically, although people say they want to have better lives, they also become so used to their difficulties that they unconsciously give up on creating a better future. They resort to platitudes such as, 'That's just how life is' or 'I guess it's my karma' instead of believing they could be happier by taking charge of their lives. If this is your unconscious attitude, you may find yourself losing focus while you do the visualization. In this case, try again but hand the resistance along with the other baggage over to the wise friend at the start of the visualization.

VISUALIZATION #9
Sensing The Future You

Play with this visualization to sense what your future self, currently hidden by all your problems, feels like. It may take several attempts to get a real sense of this; don't give up!

Stage 2 (Steps 11 to 12) is more advanced and can be practiced later. If you choose this option repeat Stage 1.

Stage 1

1. Imagine a circle of bright light in front of you. It is very sparkly and very clean.
2. You are standing outside that light on the edge of the circle.

3. See yourself as you are now. You are wearing drab and tattered clothes. These are the ones your demons have clothed your true self in. They are the fatigue, the worry, the pressure, the sense of meaninglessness, and the world-weariness. See yourself bowed under the weight of struggle, frustration, conflict or panic.
4. At your feet is a suitcase, bulging with documents that hold your outdated ideas, fears, illusions, and rigid thinking.
5. A wise and good friend comes to relieve you of this baggage. Give it over to them.
6. Now take off those grubby, smelly garments and those worn-out shoes. The wise friend offers you a white robe. Put it on or if you prefer step naked into the circle of clean, bright light in front of you.
7. Feel the light washing over you. Sense it. Let it cleanse you, this liquid sparkling light. Absorb it. Enjoy it.
8. Imagine Earth below you responds. She sends her gentle, nourishing energy up to meet that sparkling light. You are filled with dancing, radiant light.
9. Now see yourself as a candle flame at the very centre of a faceted jewel. The facets have many colors, radiating from your light.
10. What are these colors? They are your strengths, your joys, your talents, your skills, your dreams, hopes and loves.
11. Watch as the liquid light washes them clean of ingrained fear, old angers, self-doubt, objections, and self-denigration. Rest here until you are thoroughly cleansed.

Stage 2

1. Now let the scene change.
2. Imagine yourself in five, ten or twenty years. Notice that your faceted jewel has opened out like the petals of a flower. The circle of light has turned into a world that is bright, vibrant, lively and kind. It is nourishing and friendly.
3. Each facet holds a dream for yourself that has come true. In this world you are safe. You are free. You are doing all those things you love to do well. You are surrounded by people you like, respect and love just as they like, respect and love you.
4. You are a total expression of all your inner potentials. There is none other like you. You are living as your true self. Feel the wonder of this.

PART FOUR

THE PATH OF THE HEART

If I create from the heart, nearly everything works;
if from the head almost nothing.

Marc Chagall

CHAPTER 15

HEART CONSCIOUS WORK

It is only with the heart that one can see rightly;
what is essential is invisible to the eye.

Antoine de Saint-Exupery

Good Work is discovered by seeking and promoting those work experiences that generate the following qualities.

- Pleasure or upliftment
- Ease
- Engagement
- Vitality
- Balance
- Optimism
- Growth

These are the characteristics of living that are dear to the spiritual heart of you. The more you create or find them, the more your work will lead to personal success, excellence, and a contribution to others of great value, even if your job appears on the surface to be quite humble. In short, your work will work.

However, to create such work one must first be open to working with the *consciousness* that rests within the heart centre. This is not easy if a person is consumed by anxiety, resentment, boredom or hopelessness. The heart cannot easily guide those who are immersed in negativity because love and discord cannot coexist. But, even when you are committed to positive outcomes – as readers of this chapter surely are – it is highly likely that you need to learn how to find a balance within your heart consciousness when faced with a difficult situation.

The Difficulty With Finding Heart Balance

Many individuals who desire to operate from the heart will put others before themselves; the harmful effects of selfishness repel them. Yet it is a paradoxical reality that the true self can only bring the highest form of love to a situation when you regard your own well-being as equally important. This means that Good Work depends not only on loving service to others, but also on creating conditions that are self-caring at the same time. This cannot be successfully done by relying on logic or emotion alone.

Only the balance within the heart centre can find answers that ultimately work for *everyone*. Actions arising from heart consciousness are always the right ones. When the heart speaks there is a sense of mysterious certainty that comes with it. When talking to a friend about how you handled a difficult situation, you will say, 'You know, I can't explain it exactly but I just knew it was the right thing to do.' In such moments, you have a glimpse of the wisdom of the heart. It is crucial for Good Work decisions.

Unfortunately, however, the mind usually has all the clout; we are so trained in mental problem solving that most people will try to nut out what is best, weighing up the factors, rehashing old thoughts and finally making a decision that, if they were honest, is not guaranteed to bring about a greater good. The idea that they can take a step in the right direction by listening to the heart does not occur to them.

So how does one develop the skill of listening to the heart? The following visualization is a trainer-wheels exercise. It aligns the brain with heart consciousness.

Once you have learned to interpret subtle feelings or images within the heart centre, you will be able to listen to it without going through this ritual in detail. You will simply take some quiet time out to focus on the heart whenever you need it.

As with learning any language, it takes practice to get quick at understanding what is being communicated, so be patient with yourself. Don't try this exercise if you are feeling upset, angry or anxious. Wait until you have cleared those feelings.

VISUALIZATION #10
Listening To The Heart's Answers

This visualization is deeply relaxing. We suggest that you do not lie down but sit comfortably supported. If you find yourself becoming restless, stop and continue at another time when you feel calmer. Take your time with each step.

Prepare for the visualization by focusing on a situation where you are weighing up what to do. Examples: Is this a good time to approach my boss about the problem I am having with X project? Or, how should I handle a colleague to gain greater support?

If you are not certain what exact question to ask, write out as many possibilities to cover the situation. Review these questions until you sense which is the one that resonates as the most interesting or urgent.

You are now ready for the visualization.

1. Find a warm, soft place to sit where you will not be disturbed. Make yourself comfortable. Close your eyes and rest.
2. Bring to mind something you love about life. It may be something like a stranger's kindness, a friend's laugh, a favorite food or drink, or a much-loved animal. It may be an event or some activity you love. Enjoy fully these thoughts and the feelings they bring.
3. Relax now. Let outside sounds come and go. Let your mind drift. There is no hurry. These few minutes are just for you.
4. Bring your attention to yourself. Feel the air moving in and out of your nostrils. Sense the soft comfort in the surface that you rest against. Breathe in and out, dropping any tension in your jaw, shoulders, thighs and hands. You might want to stretch a bit to do so.
5. Sitting comfortably once again, breathe deeply and rest.
6. Put one hand over your heart. Feel your hand against your chest. Maybe your hand is warm; maybe it is cool. Either way is fine. Feel the beat of your heart against your hand and the rise and fall of your chest as you breathe.
7. Bring to mind once more the thing or things you love in life. Imagine these thoughts washing over you as you breathe. The warmth of these thoughts soaks down through your skin. Imagine you can feel these lovely thoughts filling you up, filling your heart.
8. Imagine the space over your heart feels expanded somehow, full of warmth.

9. Ask your heart your simple question. Let the words settle around you. Breathe and relax.
10. Feel the warmth from your hand and chest, on your out-breath. Imagine this warmth radiating outwards to wash over the question.
11. As you breathe in, imagine the answer to the question returns to you as a feeling. Explore this feeling. What does it suggest to you? For example, you might be washed with serenity or warmth and, therefore, realize that your heart agrees with your proposed plan, or you might experience the heart as hollow, and know that the heart is not in favor of it. Alternatively a definite suggestion may pop into your mind. If you are not sure of an answer, relax. It is likely that the answer will come to you over the next 24 hours.
12. Exit the visualization when you feel complete.
13. Don't forget to act on your insights. The heart is rendered powerless if you do not act on its loving recommendations.

Keeping Your Connection To Heart Consciousness Bright

Unresolved emotional discomfort always interferes with good choices and decision-making. This is why preparation for, and maintenance of, Good Work requires the *regular* use of those techniques that dissolve all forms of distress and protect you from the onslaught of negativity.

You may like to think of such routines as a daily sweeping of a golden path that is obscured by debris. Beneath this debris you will see what the next step on the path looks like, and how beautiful it is.

CHAPTER 16

YOUR AMAZING TRUE SELF STRENGTHS

If I'm going to sing like someone else,
then I don't need to sing at all.

Billie Holiday

Your talents blended with your personality strengths provide two prerequisites for Good Work: pleasure and grace. They are also intrinsic to the uniqueness of your true self's special powers that give your work a value that no one else can match or copy. They hold the flavours of love that are natural to you, and that you share most easily with others.

Regrettably, knowing and owning these strengths is much more difficult than it would first appear. There are four main reasons for this problem:

Familiarity

True self strengths and gifts are often so familiar that they don't seem special at all. How could the fact that you are naturally capable with your hands, find organizing a work event a breeze, or love giving a party be part of your spiritual talents? Lots of people do those things: surely they are insignificant?

There is a certain truth in that perception because true self capacities are often like gems in the rough that need to be identified, cut and polished.

They need effort invested in them before you see them shine. However, because they are so familiar they are often trivialized as 'just something anyone could do.' Recognizing that these easy, enjoyable capacities are *spiritual gifts* is the first step to using them in the service of Good Work.

Strangeness

Some spiritual gifts are not recognized, or even feared, because they are unusual or regarded with suspicion by your family and its culture.

As a child I discovered I had the capacity to heal with my hands. I could feel energy flowing into an injured animal, and in the case of shocked birds, was able to revive them from near death. However, since my parents - although supporting individuality in many ways - were brought up in the secular rationalism of people educated in the first half of the twentieth century, I kept this a big secret. I knew that this power would be dismissed as a sign of childish wishful thinking.

It wasn't until energy healing became accepted – together with Eastern medical practices such as acupuncture and shiatsu in the 1980s – that I admitted publicly to this strange capacity. But once I had done so this talent became a passion that led to a whole new understanding of life and became the springboard for a Good Work career. Paradoxically, if I had been born in Asia that capacity would have probably been trivialized because of its familiarity!

Judgments that wound

My reticence about owning a talent is common. We all protect ourselves from judgment and criticism by monitoring what we put out there, and in doing so often deny our genuine feelings and politically incorrect perspectives and capacities. Most people, even artists, limit the expression of their talents, airbrushing their quirky flavour for fear of the response others might have. It is not pleasant to be considered weird in some way.

Judgments that shrivel the expression of gifts are especially damaging in youth. Young people often shut down a budding talent because of parental criticism, the teasing of their peer group, or an early setback that was not handled sensitively by teachers. The world has lost the benefit of much talent due to incidents that, though minor in themselves, had terminal consequences.

Overlooking the power of your personal qualities

Of course, everyone knows that talent is a path to success, but true self strengths are more than skillfulness. Your work is given unique resonance through being imbued with positive personal qualities such as natural composure, enthusiasm, common sense or humor. It is the dynamic combination of personality strengths radiating through natural aptitudes that makes a person's work matchless and memorable.

Technique #5 and Visualization #11 below will help you appreciate your true self passions and strengths. Identifying and cultivating these self-values can lead to expanded success or be applied to finding more compatible employment.

TECHNIQUE #5
Exploring Your Self-Values

Self-values are those talents and personal qualities that you value because you can rely upon them consistently; they support or enhance your *own* well-being every time you call upon them. They are always operative in projects you enjoy.

Exercise 1: Understanding Self-Values

Using one work activity (paid or unpaid) that gives you pleasure, identify the different aspects of self that operate to create pleasure and strength in that experience.

The following dog-owner's analysis of her joyful relationship with her dog is a template.

Mental skills and knowledge: I have learned to observe my dog Bazza's communication signals, and know how to teach him tricks.

Emotional qualities: I am naturally patient with all dogs. I always find fun in dog play and training. I delight in Bazza's responsiveness.

Physical body preferences: I love running for miles in open spaces and it is great to run with Bazza when we go to my uncle's farm.

Intuitive powers: I can sometimes sense what Bazza is feeling and even thinking, as if he were speaking to me. This makes it very easy to know what to do with and for him.

Heart (spiritual) passion: I have a deep enjoyment of, and interest in, dog nature. I like to learn more about it and apply my knowledge. It makes my heart sing to I know I can give any dog a good life.

In this case, observation skills, interest in and patience for dog communication and training, enjoyment of exercise, steady appreciation of dog nature, plus the sense of personal reward in caring for dogs, are all true self strengths that could contribute to this woman being a successful and inspired worker or owner in a dog business: her own form of Good Work.

Exercise 2: Developing a Statement of Self-Values

Now take time to draw up a general list of your Self-Values by observing your mental skills, knowledge and interests, positive emotional qualities, physical body's capacities, and your intuitive powers as they show up in all aspects of your life: not just your current job.

The Statement of Self-Values is a reference point for creating Good Work because any kind of activity that utilizes them will be enjoyable.

Keep the Statement where you can add to it over time. Even if you cannot find paid work that suits these strengths right now look for ways to continue to exercise them. They will always lead you to greater self-empowerment. They enhance your entire life.

Note carefully: The Statement Of Self-Values is not a catalogue of what others regard as your strengths. A typical example might be that you are well known for your kindness and your skill in carpentry, which you employ to make toys to give away to needy children. However, before you can include kindness and carpentry in your Statement you need to ask yourself, are you actually kind to *yourself*? Do *you* really enjoy carpentry? You need to ask yourself if the observed characteristic enhances your own life as well as others.

The Relationship Of Love To Action

You will see from the example of the dog trainer that there is a close connection between giving to the animal she loves and receiving enjoyment from the many activities that are part of her relationship with him. True self strengths are not necessarily remarkable in themselves; it is when they combine to create love for both yourself and another that they become special.

In short, you are always practicing Good Work when your work is characterized by the cycle of giving love to something and *at the same time* receiving love from it.

VISUALIZATION #11
Connecting The Heart's Love To Practical Action

This visualization strengthens your mental and emotional understanding of the relationship between something you value and your loving behaviors and attitudes towards it. Equally important, it illustrates how such engagement is repaid by more love and pleasure.

1. Go to your Inner Garden of Serenity and Well-Being. (Visualization #1, How To Use This Book.)
2. Imagine that your higher self or a wise friend comes to assist you to learn more of your true self nature.
3. Breathe in light from above your head through the crown and then take it down to focus on the centre of the chest: the place of heart consciousness.
4. Place your hand over this point.
5. Take time to breathe into the heart. Gradually connect to the calm that is within the heart.
6. Relax fully. Let images arise of three activities in your life that you really enjoy. These can be physical, emotional, mental or spiritual in nature.
7. Choose the one that offers the strongest impression. Recall the experience fully. What kind of nourishment does it provide? How does it offer you such things as pleasure, comfort, upliftment, safety, or the wonder of beauty?

8. Keep your awareness on the heart centre. Fill it with light. Extend the heart vibration outward to flow over this valued thing.
9. Ask yourself what you do to actively show that you love and value these things? For example, if you love your car, you may spend time polishing it and maintaining it. If it is a child, you may ensure that she has a stimulating education through sharing your interests. If it is your garden you may spend time tending it, appreciating it or studying its changing seasons.
10. Remember the pleasure you have in these activities. Notice how your mind, your emotions, your body and life energy are engaged in them.
11. You now have a sense of how the love in the heart is made real by the loving actions you take to sustain the thing you love, and the pleasure you get from that participation. You are in touch with the grand value of your true self strengths.

CHAPTER 17

THE POWER OF PURPOSE

Life is an opportunity to create meaning. Meaning has not to be discovered: it has to be created. You will find meaning only if you create it.... It is not there like a rock that you will find. It is a poetry to be composed, it is a song to be sung, it is a dance to be danced.[1]

Osho

In my youth I spent time in the United Kingdom working as a temporary office worker. In a letter to my family I describe an all-too-common problem that, then as now, contributes to bad work: the fact that a particular job lacks any inner meaning for the worker.

'There is a youngish fellow in our office who is supposedly learning cost estimation. He spends half the day doodling, yawning and doing things twice over. Poor guy is intolerably bored, and he sadly reflected the other day that he wished there were a pill he could take

1 Osho cited http://worldbeyond.org/quotes.htm

every morning that would allow him to find himself awake at 5 p.m. with all the work done, and time to go home.'

As the apprentice estimator's plight shows, a meaningless job is agonizing because it has no shape, point or direction. Lack of meaning drains work of drive and commitment, and therefore pleasure. Without any purpose at all you are in a boat bobbing endlessly on an open sea, and liable to spiritual starvation with its despair, resentment and self-dislike.

However, when a particular worker endures a sense of meaninglessness, the problem is not the employer's responsibility to solve. A job description, though it implies a purpose for the business, does not guarantee experiences that your true self finds valuable. Therefore, creating a personal reason for any work activity is something only you can do. Wresting purpose from a less than satisfactory job rests with your willingness to drop your dependence on hand-me-down motivations and look for opportunities to find meaning for yourself.

In short, responsibility for your own work purposes cannot be handballed to someone else; these must be found by deciding what emotional value you can manufacture out of your immediate challenges. Even a short term and seemingly trivial purpose provides a context for you to usefully learn more about yourself, to gain an unexpected competence, or to engage in life in unplanned ways.

As this advice may seem rather abstract, here is an example from my experience of housework: which I find tedious in the extreme.

Having a picture-perfect house is not particularly important to me; I tend to put off housework until a tipping point is reached in the form of the layers of dust and piles of scattered items that accumulate over too many days.

Faced with the necessity of preparing a little-used and, therefore, poorly tended room for a party, I decided to give myself the goal of not only cleaning it thoroughly but making it look as fabulous as possible in as short a time as possible. House decoration, unlike house maintenance, is one of my pleasures. Not surprisingly, the work was great fun, time flew by without a whiff of tedium, and the final result met with many compliments.

I used my true self's creative streak to give enjoyment to an original purpose that was unappealing. Of course, I could have employed a cleaner for the day, but giving myself a purpose I found more emotionally and mentally entertaining than cleaning was far more rewarding.

The Danger Of Myths About What Work Is Good

Only a minority of individuals invents ways out of meaninglessness or tedium. Most cannot do this effectively because their dreams rely on myths about what kind of work is significant or joyful.

They fantasize about how, one day, they will win a lottery so they can give up their day job to spend their time on their hobbies for which they have passion. They imagine that Good Work will be fired by unflagging commitment, always seem like play, or be a spectacularly successful venture.

These myths are, for the most part, a dangerous distraction from creating personal meaning because you will discount any experience that does not align with them; consequently, you will be blind to opportunities that suit your true self's nature.

Myths are also dangerous even when people are relatively happy in their work activities; they have doubts that their work is right for them because it seems to lack some important spiritual element. They ask questions such as: What am I here for? How do I know I am making the right choices? What does God want from me? The majority of people believe that knowing the answer to these questions will automatically give them a sense of satisfaction.

Spiritually speaking, it is true that your life has broader purposes. Knowing the bigger picture is a wonderful thing, but hard to pinpoint if you are mesmerized by the myth that spiritual purposes are spectacular.

Those who believe they lack spiritual purpose usually see the word purpose spelt with a capital P. Subconsciously they believe that purpose is the result of a calling from God to do righteous work or the expression of rare talent. Purpose of this kind is steeped in missionary zeal whereby a grand outcome is achieved: you are Joan of Arc saving your nation from evil domination by foreigners, or uncovering an instant cure for drug addiction, or saving the environment single-handedly.

One's own life purposes are not necessarily particularly elevated or visible to others. Rather they can best be identified by those small, immediate experiences that offer you a feeling of upliftment, or to which you are magnetically drawn over and over in different ways: pursuits that give loving service in simple ways, that enlighten you, that create beauty or order, or bring healing or fun to ordinary life. No aspect of life is too trivial, ordinary, or even painful for it to qualify as having the potential for spiritual purpose.

A person's spiritual purposes cannot be described in simple terms nor are they downloaded in singular insights or dramatic events; when such exciting revelations do occur they are only pointers to the way ahead. The intricacy of spiritual purpose is uncovered throughout one's life in themes of repeated experience that weave a complex fabric of wisdom and greater self-empowerment.

The Many Faces Of Purpose

Spiritual myths about work generally suggest that purpose has a singular, unchanging focus. In reality, purpose is multi-dimensional and evolves as your interests and concerns change and as you age. Purpose always moves;

it moves daily and even hour-by-hour. Here are some examples of different kinds of purpose, all of which are equally valid in Good Work.

- It is for immediate or long-term economic survival or prosperity.
- It is an exercise in strengthening your talents or self-confidence.
- It is a necessary building block for a future goal.
- You are doing it solely for the pleasure it gives you.
- It is supporting the welfare of others you genuinely care about.
- It's for personal growth via exposure to new experiences and learning.
- It is to provide an opportunity to express mastery of your craft.

As you may deduce from this list, your occupation may cover several or all of these purposes. From the point of view of your spiritual self, none of them are any less or more legitimate than the others, whatever society might say. However, the purposes that the true self most enjoys are those that actively create ease, pleasure and/or growth no matter what your age or circumstance.

Reflection

Take a moment to reflect on a work activity you have been undertaking recently. Where does it fit into the categories of purpose listed above?

How are you to know if those purposes are 'right'?

Hint: The answer rests with your emotions and the body. Did the activity give you a sense of physical, mental or emotional pleasure or relief? Did it promote inner peace, inspiration, connection or simple bodily satisfaction?

It is your emotional state, rather than your thoughts alone, that give the clearest indication that your true self is satisfied by the purpose you have given it.

Beyond Conscious Purpose

Notwithstanding what I have said about spiritual purposes often being hidden from view, readers of this book are likely to want to know that their work is spiritually aligned with the bigger picture.

For such people, it is worrying when one feels one might be off track. However, this concern may be quite unfounded because the conscious mind's understanding of life purposes is very limited.

Even when a particular goal is aligned with one's gifts, the project in itself may not be its real spiritual purpose. Sometimes a job is simply an avenue to broader growth that is not anticipated by your conscious mind.

This point is illustrated by one of our students. R's musicianship is a spiritual gift to which he gives specific purposes.

> *'My goal for 2013 was to release a record, to step out into the wider world with my creative endeavors and to plant something out there for people to interact with.*
>
> *This expansion inevitably meant working with many people along the way: developing an audience and communicating with them, bringing in other creators and facilitators, and reaching out to form relationships with others in the industry.*
>
> *It's this aspect of my achievement that I am most proud of as it has led to a strong sense of self-trust and a greater awareness of my core strengths. Perhaps the most valuable lesson I've learnt is to trust in decisions spawned from positive emotional resonance, and to pursue those opportunities which feel good or develop with ease. These were the ones that led to personal success at a pace that was comfortable.'*

This man's experience is a beautiful example of how using a spiritual talent to create a dream led to his exploration of new relationship processes that gave him a greater appreciation of his true self and how to succeed.

It was not the conscious purpose to which he put his gift that revealed the plan his true self had for him but what he learned along the way.

Conscious reflection on what you learn from experience is often the most certain way to know what your spiritual purpose is about because, over time, certain themes will reveal themselves. In the case of the musician, it is clear that self-trust and working with others are important to his soul growth.

CHAPTER 18

CREATIVE BALANCE: A MUST-HAVE ABILITY

Let us note that art ... has never been confined to 'idea';
art has always been the 'realized' expression of equilibrium.

Piet Mondrian

Good Work depends on creative balance: a balance between imagining an inspired future and the practical action needed to make the possibility real.

If a dynamic balance is not struck between your working life dreams and the flexible actions needed to implement them, the dreams themselves cannot be realized.

Creating such balance is complex because it requires continual adjustment. However, it is made a whole lot easier when the right and left hemispheres of the brain operate cooperatively to both inspire and also surmount the real life obstacles associated with making one's job both agreeable and effective.

Unfortunately, however, this is where the first and most important imbalance occurs: most individuals use their creative consciousness in an unbalanced way. Some people prefer right brain imaginative functions to fire their engagement with their work; others rely heavily on left-brain 'can do' competencies to achieve desired outcomes.

Knowing Your Creative Style

Fiona and I have dubbed these two different approaches as characteristic of right brain orientated 'Sky' or left-brain orientated 'Earth' personalities. Although every individual has access to the capacities of the least preferred hemisphere, the preference for one style of thinking over the other leads to different value systems and also different limitations that affect how work an individual can make their work Good.

Each type downplays or ignores the importance of the less-preferred hemisphere's contribution to the power of their work. Good Work, however, needs both: a personal vision or dream for one's work combined with practical competencies that are strong enough to negotiate the frustrations of real world limitations, and especially those that arise from interpersonal interactions.

Read the following information with an eye to working out which polarity you are likely to be.

Sky Personality Consciousness

Sky's positive attributes

People who view life and its challenges through a right brain perspective are often considered creative because they enjoy discovering new knowledge and giving birth to original perspectives. They prefer activities that involve research into the unknown, big picture innovation, artistic pursuits, and mysticism. Imagination and abstract thinking are their specialties.

The Sky personality has personal preferences associated with right-brain expansiveness. Sky people are freedom loving, adventurous and trusting of universal abundance. They like to do their own thing and dislike feeling constricted. When a person is in Sky mode, he or she is a dreamer who flies above the terrain of ordinary life in search of future knowledge, future powers and grand solutions. The positive Sky speaks with authority and pithy accuracy. It knows what is true and what is not. When Sky raises its energetic frequency, it is the source of divine inspiration. It is out of this consciousness that great leaps in human knowledge and understanding are made.

Sky's negative characteristics

On the other hand, in its negative aspect Sky can be confused, overwhelmed and fragmented as one idea follows too quickly on the heels of another. In its extreme form, too many projects are accepted, then abandoned or never satisfactorily completed. A rosy but unrealistic glow surrounds grand plans, which are fantasies rather than genuine potentials.

Alternatively, in an attempt to anchor their ideas, Sky individuals may fix upon their creative ideas with a perfectionist rigidity that prevents them becoming viable in the real world. Inflexibility and closed-mindedness are qualities associated with a negative Sky approach to getting things done. They are not necessarily impractical, however, because in some areas of daily life where they are most interested they will be quite organized and effective.

Most problems that Sky individuals face are due to the fact that Sky relationship skills are relatively weaker than their Earth partners. When they are under stress Sky people's capacity to work with others goes out the window because they are easily overwhelmed by the emotionality of other people.

Sky personalities respond to this anxiety by becoming aloof and unrelated, or they may appear arrogant in their convictions. A Sky leader will have to work hard at getting others on board because they take the attitude that 'It's my way or the highway.'

Faced with revolt, Sky people become so frustrated with other people that they resort to mental head butting or they withdraw emotionally altogether. They indulge in blame games. But underneath that response is a profound anxiety that they have little value because the impact of their work is less significant than they want it to be.

Naturally, these negativities do not show up all the time! Sky people are often lighthearted, witty, and fun to be with. Sky extroverts have sparkly personalities that are powerful in those professions where presentation is important. At its best, Sky's sense of humor and uniqueness makes for a very interesting and engaging companion.

The Task Of Balance For The Sky Personality

The task for the Sky personality is to identify and honor their self-expressive powers and at the same time release their inner anxieties and their judgments about other people. Learning effective interpersonal communication skills so that they can be heard is important. Above all, they need to learn as many ways as possible to ensure that they pace themselves, and do not become overwhelmed by work demands. The more tangible competencies a Sky individual can acquire, the more secure they will feel.

Earth Personality Consciousness

Earth's positive qualities

Left-brain orientated individuals are appreciated as reliable, dogged workers, putting more value on making something happen rather than dreaming up a new possibility. For this reason they are regarded as less creative than Sky people. In fact this is not necessarily so, but their creativity is of a different kind. Earth's creativity is demonstrated in how they work with human and material limitations in a common sense, mix-and-match way. Earth people do not believe that they must win the lottery to fulfill their dreams. They are happy to get what they want on a budget or by working in a step-by-step way to prosperity.

The Earth perspective in its positive aspect is less inspiring than Sky but it is likely to be more successful in work projects because the relationship implications are taken into account. Earth's heart rests in what will create an abundant sense of physical comfort and well-being for all those it cares for. These are the healers and servants of the world. They are friendly, warm and reliable people.

For this reason, though the Earth perspective may lack originality and keep low to the ground, there is an immense comfort in knowing that its practicality will feed the body and provide the warmth needed for life in the here-and-now. The left-brain with its boundaries, its step-by-step thinking, and its harmonizing flexibility has the great advantage of transforming energy into tangible success that others appreciate.

Earth's negative characteristics

Unfortunately, because Earth values life as it is, it is conservative by nature and it will greatly fear dreams or expression of the true self that is likely to cause disruption or change the status quo. While Sky loves freedom, Earth loves security. This love of security is excessive: it fears people's disapproval, financial loss and taking risks on new ventures.

When Earth's concerns are threatened, it becomes nitpicking, pessimistic and burdened. Its practicality becomes a wet blanket for wonderful dreams: it always has a reason why not. The concern for others turns into a form of emotional control rather than an expression of love. Negative Earth attitudes tend to martyrhood, and in this it can become self-righteously supportive of dysfunctional relationships. Although Earth tolerates bad behaviour for a long time, when pressed too far, an Earth person may snap in a manner that is shocking because it seems out of character.

Earth ignores the true self when it works out of obligation rather than enjoyment.

Unfortunately, though Earth truly wants the best for everyone, its willingness to stand up for what is right for its true self is weakened by the fear that by rocking the boat relationship harmony will be lost. They do not know how to set boundaries that support their own needs. Because of these fears, Earth people narrow their capacity for enjoyment to those activities that serve others. Their unique forms of self-expression rarely see the light of day. Taking a walk on the wild side of creativity is not for them.

The Task Of Balance For Earth Personalities

Earth individuals are too earnest. Under stress, they overwork rather than take a holiday. To a stressful situation they add more stress and more work. When this happens, they abandon fun, inspiration and humor: which they usually delegate to their Sky partners! They do not like to admit their anger so instead they often resort to being passively aggressive rather than openly asking for what they need. Learning to set boundaries is an important self-development task for these folk.

Earth personalities are risk-adverse and cling on to self-denying situations far too long. They need to let go of control and to develop a trust in the higher self and their gut instincts. Earth balance is assured when they can let go of obligations and exercise their right to me-time pleasure and creative self-expression.

Reflection

On the basis of the descriptions of Sky and Earth consciousness, which do you most identify with? In what situations do you tend to be more like the other kind of personality?

Bringing Balance To Your Creative Personality Style

You are likely to identify with both aspects of Earth and Sky in your own personality. However, although these polarities are inherent in each of us, when you are under stress the negative aspects of your personality style will come to the fore. At such times, your limitations will undermine your chances of creating or maintaining Good Work.

All visualizations in this book have the effect of improving creative balance, but they work more effectively if the brain is physiologically primed for it. The following two visualizations are brain gym techniques to help physiological flow. You must do Visualization 12 A before you attempt 12 B.

VISUALIZATION #12A
Brain Balancing Exercise No.1

Practicing this technique helps you to flow your consciousness between the functions of both right and left hemispheres of the brain with equal ease. Even if you have used similar exercises before, practice it for 1- 2 weeks. At first it is likely to feel awkward. Do not struggle with it. Keep your practice very short but return to it until it becomes smooth and easy.

You may worry that you are not visualizing the figure of eight in the correct position in your brain. Don't be concerned; your unconscious mind will adjust the flow of energy to fit what is required.

1. Close your eyes and relax fully.
2. Focus your attention just above your nose. Imagine a figure of 8 (or infinity sign) lying horizontally between the two brain hemispheres but deep enough to sit between the ears.

This is where the band that is the cross-point of the hemispheres, the corpus callosum, is located.

3. Visualize that the figure of 8 is lit up. Imagine a small, brighter point of light moving around the horizontal figure of 8 from one side of the brain to the other.
4. As it travels, see the figure of 8 getting brighter and bigger, and the point of light flowing more and more smoothly.
5. Play with the image, allowing it to enlarge to fill the entire brain. Use different colors of your choice.
6. Maintain this practice for a very short time for the first practice: ten seconds is enough. Then extend it slowly, little by little, each day for 7 – 14 days or until the flow between the two sides of the brain feels smooth. *Only practice this technique for as long as it feels comfortable.*

VISUALIZATION #12B
Brain Balancing Exercise No. 2

Having worked on the basic brain balance for at least a week, you may like to balance the brain forward and backwards. This connects your physicality to your spirituality.

1. Relax. Move into working Brain Balance 1 until you feel the energy is smooth.
2. Imagine that this balance is continuing as you proceed to the next step.

3. See your head in profile. Visualize a figure of 8 flowing from the forehead to the back of the brain and then forward again.
4. Work the figure of eight, allowing it to grow brighter and clearer as the pinpoint of light moves around it.
5. Practice this visualization for 1-2 weeks and then from time to time as you sense you need it.

CHAPTER 19

CREATING OPPORTUNITIES

A pessimist sees the difficulty in every opportunity;
an optimist sees the opportunity in every difficulty.
Winston Churchill

Good Work often depends on actively looking for and making the most of opportunities.

I had a Good Work turning point when I changed my career from teaching to counseling. During the transition I needed a job that would give me a bridging income. As I was studying intensively, the job could not be too demanding of my time and energy and yet it had to supply me with adequate funds.

Fortunately, the facilitators who had introduced me to the concept of the Wheel of Life Balance (Chapter 8) had suggested that in choosing work of any kind, including part-time or occasional work, one had to look for the potential for genuine pleasure in it. Financial necessity, they said, had to be balanced with enjoyment: a notion I thought very radical indeed, but one I later learned is central to Good Work. This meant that part-time teaching was not an option; that was a case of same ol' and I knew only too well how tiring and emotionally unsatisfying it would be.

However, applying the Good Work principle of enjoyment to opportunities while covering survival necessities can be daunting. Where do you find such work? What does it look like? How will you negotiate your requirements? There is no big neon sign in the sky pointing to the perfect opportunity. Interviews with prospective employers rarely help because they investigate how your skills will serve the business, rather than how the job might suit your Good Work criteria. It's easy to forget the Good Work plan and end up taking whatever job is on offer.

The best way to prevent expediency overtaking your decisions is to prepare a checklist of Good Work requirements. This checklist provides an invaluable reference for assessing any opportunity to see if it suits the mental, emotional, physical and spiritual aspects of your true self. The brainstorming exercise that follows, *The Working Life Wish List*, does this. It also ensures creative balance because it uses both right and left hemispheres of the brain.

It is important to feel excited about creating a new opportunity at the time you draw up this Wish List. If you are not genuinely interested in changing jobs, wait until you are. The exercise depends for its effectiveness on a strong motivation to make a practical change.

You will need a pen and paper and a countdown timer.

TECHNIQUE #6
The Working Life Wish List

Step 1: Preparation

Read the instructions here carefully at least twice. The details are important.

Set a timer for 20 minutes.

Step 2: Brainstorming

Make a list of 40 conditions that would create a perfect working life within the 20-minute time limit. Make sure that you do not confine your thinking to the practical or realistic. Allow for the bigger dreams as well as trivial details. Let your dreams be as expansive and emotional as you can make them: just so long as you would genuinely like each item. Keep forcing yourself to think of new things, even down to the color of the room you would like to work in!

Step 3: Decide your basic needs

Read the list over to identify 4 single conditions that cover your essential needs.

These four items are your top survival priorities because they will provide *basic security and practicality*. Examples: A job will have to pay your basic bills if you have no other source of income; if you have no car, it will need to be within easy reach of public transport, etc. Make sure these items genuinely are essential and no cutting back, compromise or alternative solution is possible. These are the rock-bottom survival items that your practical left-brain Earth self has facts at hand to prove you absolutely cannot do without.

Many people find Step 3 is difficult because the items have to be expressed in a very precise way. It is not sufficient to say you wish to have 'an income to cover basic needs.' Instead an essential item, such as income, must be expressed in tangible terms, that is, as the dollars per week that you have *checked out* are necessary to cover survival costs you cannot avoid. Of course, you will no doubt be happy to receive more than a basic living wage, but the figure you fix upon is a bottom line that can be used to assess new possibilities in a brutally realistic light.

Step 4: Review your 4 essentials

Will your mind, body and emotions be happy with these? If not, consider replacing one item with another from your brainstorming list. Note: It is not important if your heart's passions are not included in these essentials.

Step 5: Identify the 4 most thrilling desires

Select 4 single features of a job that would thrill you. These are your bliss items; they would give you *great joy and/or freedom.* They do not have to seem probable or practical. They are not necessarily things you can negotiate or guarantee. However, remember they are genuine dreams for work, not fantasies. These appeal to the right brain Sky aspect of self. Your heart will have a say in choosing these items. Examples: I am working with a wonderful boss; I travel the world exploring my greatest interest.

Step 6: Review your lists carefully and adjust until you are happy with your final 8 items: 4 for essential, 4 for bliss.

Warning! Make sure you haven't cheated by including more than one feature in each point. This is a common mistake. Example: I want to earn a good wage that supports my family, *but does not exhaust me*. The italicized requirement should be allocated to a separate point.

Step 7: Put this list, which is a balanced framework for considering job opportunities, where you can refer to it easily.

Following Through With Your Wish List

At this point, you should have a clearer picture of how you want your working life to be in the foreseeable future. You are on the way to creating an environment that supports Good Work. Now is the time to take one step towards making it happen.

The reality is that at this point you are likely to balk. You may say that no job could actually allow for such a range of delights, and you will give up before you have started. However, *The Working Life Wish List* is just that; it is the picture of what you want to create, not a description of a particular job.

In other words, the wish list may have to be achieved step-by-step by looking for opportunities to meet your desired conditions, and negotiating each of them until they become a reality over time. Sometimes these opportunities can be negotiated in your current employment; some may have to be found in a new job or multi-stream incomes.

It is easy to be daunted by the degree of persistence this process requires; however, it can be speeded up if you use your intuitive capacity to uncover or explore opportunities with the assistance of your higher self. (See Day 8, A 10-Day Course In Making Daily Work Good.)

To provide evidence of the power of the Wish List, here is my own example of how I applied it.

My bridging job had to have the following four essentials: enough money to pay basic bills; allow enough time for study, that is, it had to be part-time; did not require long-term commitment since I planned to leave in two years; and, finally, used skills I already had.

My four bonus items were that the job would involve me in a project I felt inspired by, give me work with a friendly, professional team of equals, allow me to choose what times I worked, and offer opportunities for influence.

How unlikely is it that a part-time worker could possibly expect such a miracle to eventuate? However, I obtained every item on my wish list! But not instantly. These conditions were gradually met because I kept an eye out for wish list opportunities and negotiated my way to them from an unlikely beginning.

My first step was a phone call, not to seek paid employment but to offer my skills as a volunteer. The particular non-profit organization I chose offered the chance to participate in an innovative educational project I was enthusiastic about. Although I was initially asked to handle simple clerical jobs, within three days the committee chairman asked me to join the project's steering committee because of my school experience. Bingo! I had a project I was interested in, tasks that fitted my experience, and a position of influence.

Soon came opportunities for paid administrative work on the project. This was within my skillset as I have qualifications in business studies. I negotiated a job setting up a small office on terms that, after several detours, covered all my financial necessities, plus the right to work part-time hours when I wanted. Although the personal influence aspect changed its nature when I became employed, I retained it in the form of being responsible for project review.

This is not to say that I managed all these things without support. I remember with the greatest affection and respect the wonderful leader of that group who allowed me such freedom. It is not surprising that he had been the chief executive officer of a highly successful corporation. He allowed people their Good Work. You will find that the Universe brings such people to if you are genuinely committed to having what you want.

Notwithstanding this story of possibility, and a clear sense of what you should do to move forward, you are still likely to resist acting on your wish list. You are likely to have a whole lot of 'Yes, buts...' rattling around in your head. Pessimism will take over, or perfectionism that refuses to consider any job unless it ticks every single box.

This is where you will have to take charge of yourself. You must commit to just one step towards Good Work.

Read over your list and consider what action you could take to get the ball rolling. Do you need to do some research? Speak to someone? Clear an anxiety or negative beliefs? It does not matter if this action seems quite insignificant, so long as it is intended as the first step of a series.

Overcoming Resistance To Action

Surprising though it seems, the choice to create more well-being automatically brings resistance. Change is always resisted as a form of protection: even change for the better. This protective tension originates at a mental and/or emotional level although it always shows itself physically as well. People freeze, procrastinate, find excuses, or become stubborn about not listening to or acting upon their wisdom.

The following visualization releases resistance to acting on a choice. Letting go of resistance allows you to move forward with ease and common sense. Use this visualization every time you put off doing something that you know is necessary for your welfare. (Dental appointments are good practice!)

VISUALIZATION #13
Releasing Resistance And Procrastination

1. Find a comfortable, uninterrupted space to sit or lie down. Ensure your body is warm and well supported.
2. Close your eyes gently. Relax your whole body as best you can. Let your breathing become a fraction deeper and slower.
3. Imagine that you are transported to a most beautiful garden, secluded and safe. It is late summer in your Garden of Serenity and Well-Being. The sun is gently warm. The shade under the trees is pleasantly cool.
4. Look around this garden. What do you see? Tall leafy shrubs? Roses? A small vegetable garden with herbs? Fruit trees with sweet fruit? Maybe there is a fishpond or small fountain? This garden is magical.
5. Enjoy the colors. Smell the fragrant air. Flowers and fruit seem to invite you to touch them, to smell them, and taste them. Take your time. Wander around this garden, sensing it and enjoying it.
6. Now find a place to sit comfortable or to lie down. Imagine you are doing that. Do you see yourself doing that? Or do you prefer to feel yourself in that position? Make a choice based on which is most easy for you: seeing or feeling.
7. Begin to observe or sense the points of tension in your body that arise from the resistance or procrastination you are experiencing. Notice where that is? Your stomach? Your

shoulders? Your jaw? Neck? Hands? Let your awareness move over your whole body.

8. Pretend now that the earth below you is magically drawing this tension down and away. Relax even more as the earth draws this tension away.
9. Now you see or feel a bubble around you. It is comfortable inside the bubble: it is your personal space bubble and it is the place of your current experience of work. Despite its discomforts, the familiarity of this space makes it paradoxically quite tolerable.
10. Around the bubble is a skin, a skin that is protecting you. But you notice that it is slightly murky, or it seems to be distorting the view. From inside this bubble you cannot see the garden as well as you would like to. You know nothing out there is ugly or frightening. There is no need to protect yourself from it. Everything is beautiful.
11. You decide you would like to release this skin so that you can enjoy the garden more, and see it more clearly. Make sure you make this choice with firm commitment.
12. Place your hands on the skin or shell of the bubble. Let it melt away. Perhaps you want to break it gently. Whatever you choose, make it happen with your will.
13. As you step beyond the bubble, stretch out your hand to touch something you saw earlier in the garden. Notice it is far more radiant, more vivid than before.
14. Then you notice something even more wonderful. You notice you, too, are more radiant, more alive, and more clear in mind and heart. You feel free, safe and able to move with greater ease and impact. Exit when you are ready.

Once you have completed this visualization, act immediately. If you still can't act, you need to consider if the goal you set yourself was not timely, is too big a step to manage, or too frightening. In Part 5 you will find answers to these problems.

CHAPTER 20

REVIEW: YOUR FORMULA FOR SUCCESS

When love and skill work together, expect a masterpiece.

John Ruskin

Parts One to Four are designed to give you a general understanding of the main Good Work principles. These can be summarized as follows: Good Work is based in the *expression of your true self aptitudes and interests* in an activity that has *personal meaning* for you and where you *create an internal environment* that allows you to *stay in charge of making your work as holistically enjoyable and comfortable as possible.*

Now is the moment to draw the threads together so that you can begin living these principles on a daily basis. The skills for making your daily work Good are explored in Part Five.

However, the following optional review is an entertaining way to record and apply your current understanding of the Good Work principles to a real life situation. It provides a map of your journey to Good Work so far. It shows you at what points in that journey you have less competence.

Make sure you choose a time where you don't feel pressured. Better not to do this exercise at all than hurry it.

TECHNIQUE #7
A Map For The Adventure

Step 1: Choose A Focus For Investigation

Choose an immediate goal that relates to a private work project. The more specific the goal is, the more useful this exercise will be. Example: 'Autumn renovation of my garden' has better focus than 'Creating a beautiful garden' because this goal can be achieved in a short time; it is not overwhelmingly large or long term.

To make your project one that your heart agrees with, close your eyes, place your hand over your chest, and ask what project you would like to get underway. Let ideas float into your mind until one feels right. Don't force it; it has to be something you genuinely want to do.

Step 2: Preparation

Set aside at least an hour for this exercise. This time can be broken into shorter more convenient intervals if you wish.

Make sure you have a quiet workspace with room enough for drawing.

Collect a large sheet of newsprint and some colored pens. Note: Even if you feel uncomfortable with drawing, have a go. Pretend you are back in kindergarten so that you do not feel too serious about it.

Write the name of your project at the top of the paper. Draw lines dividing the paper down the centre and also across the middle so that you have four equal quadrants.

Number the quadrants and label them as follows.

Quadrant 1 Bottom left: Where I Am Right Now

Quadrant 2 Top right: My Dream

Quadrant 3 Bottom right: My Powers

Quadrant 4 Top left: My Formula for Success

Step 3: Fill In Quadrant #1: Where I Am Right Now

Using your colored pens, draw a small figure to represent yourself. A stick figure will be fine if you are no artist. But make sure you give the figure clothes, facial features etc. Don't be tempted to use the black pen for this figure!

Draw two large bubbles of different colours to fill the rest of the space. Connect one bubble to your heart, one to your head.

In the heart bubble, write notes about the positives in your plan. Example: Have Saturday afternoon off to do this project, beautiful weather, getting help of my friend, love pruning, looking forward to making new compost bin.

In the head bubble, write down any concerns you have, including any worries about the next step to take. Examples: A lot to do, not a lot of time, need to spend money on it but have other commitments.

Add any extra features, such as a frown or a smile on your figure, illustrate your current state of mind.

Step 4: Fill In Quadrant #2: My Dream

Draw a scene to represent the dream you have for this project with as many stick figures as necessary, yourself included, of course. Take your time with this illustration. Make sure you have covered every feature of the dream. Again use plenty of colors.

Add emoticons or labels to indicate how you and others

would feel about the successful completion of this project or goal. Examples: Relaxed, admiring, enthusiastic, grateful, relieved.

Step 5: Fill In Quadrant #3: My Powers

Draw a large stick figure of yourself wearing a crown for conscious thought, and holding a magic wand for transforming inner limitations. At your feet, draw a toolbox of the competencies, skills or actions that you will use to create success. Examples: Research building a compost bin; buy better secateurs; clear stress before starting work.

Step 6: Review Your Progress To This Point

Which quadrant from 1 – 3 did you find it the hardest or least appealing to fill in? Which illustration seems the least confidently expressed? Where is color lacking? The weakest quadrant indicates where you need more focus in order to create Good Work.

Step 7: Fill In Quadrant #4: My Formula For Success

Draw colored rungs of a ladder to fill this space. You can fill these in as you proceed with your project or it can be completed as a post-project reflection. They should include every aspect used to complete this project to your satisfaction.

All the skills and actions you use to complete your project: ability to dig, carpentry skills, landscape designing, IT research to find extra information on soil compost heaps.

All the personality attributes that help you to enjoy it: physical strength for the job, eye for design, love of vegetables, eye for detail.

All personality characteristics that cause you to feel frustrated: impatience with weeding, irritation with 'helper', getting distracted by talking to neighbor.

All the ways you overcame inner anxieties and the frustrations. Think beyond whatever we have suggested here to any personal growth technique that works for you.

Any other insight relevant to creating Good Work experiences.

Strengthening The Weakest Area In Your Formula: Some Suggestions

- Quadrant 1 indicates that unconscious fears about the work itself, such as getting it wrong or its being beyond your capacity, are affecting your motivation. Use Visualization #13, *Releasing Resistance And Procrastination*, Chapter 19. If you can identify the anxieties, clear them with Visualization #15, *The Jell-O Wall* in Day 1, A 10-Day Course In Making Daily Work Good.
- Quadrant 2 shows you need to develop your capacity to dream. This problem often indicates a belief that imagination or dreaming will get out of control so that you will become ungrounded. Use Visualization #3, *Changing A Mental Belief*, Chapter 2 to change this negative belief. Practice creating small dreams to increase your self-confidence.
- Quadrant 3 difficulties mean that you tend to be overwhelmed by the task. Recall Technique #5, *Exploring Your Self-Values*, Chapter 16. Use it to remind yourself of the particular strengths or skills you have in regard to this particular project. Do you need to develop more skills in order to feel competent?
- Finally: Failure to fill in Quadrant 4 indicates that you are resistant to this analysis. Some people find mental analysis uncomfortable; however, it is possible that the project you chose was not one that your heart was really interested in. Or are you influenced by an inner saboteur that is unwilling or frightened to put energy into analyzing exactly how you could be more successful?

PART FIVE

A 10-DAY COURSE IN MAKING DAILY WORK GOOD

Yesterday is history, tomorrow is a mystery, today is God's gift, that's why we call it the present.

Joan Rivers

CHAPTER 21

INTRODUCTION TO THE COURSE

Life is trying things to see if they work.

Ray Bradbury[1]

In the previous sections of this book, we introduced the key principles that underpin the ability to create Good Work. These remain the same no matter who you are or what your situation is. Once you have a grasp of these concepts, you are ready to benefit by A 10-day Course In Making Daily Work Good, which shows you how to embody the skills for Good Working on a daily basis. Mastery of these skills not only gives spiritual radiance to your projects but also gives you strength to address challenges.

The Course has two aims: Encouraging you to experiment until your true self is better served, and strengthening your ability to handle the rub of working life.

If you believe you are not yet ready to develop these skills, you will still find value in reading those topics that resonate with you.

1 http://thinkexist.com/quotes/like/life_is-trying_things_to_see_if_they_work/339281/

Strengthening Your Ability To Support Your Heart Conscious Projects In Daily Life

As Good Work springs from your spiritually aligned self, it is naturally blessed; your life energy and your heart's desire flow easily to it. This makes the fundamental power and authenticity of your work indisputable.

However, Good Work is also a major avenue for your participation in the community and life itself. And herein lies the difficulty. Each of us operates in the context of uncertain and ever changing conditions, as well as other people's insecurities and perspectives. Too many external difficulties are likely to cause you to slowly lose belief in your true self's power, and with that loss, the desire to continue. This can be very painful. Hopelessness leads to the resentment, self-dislike and disappointment that failure brings.

Therefore, the greatest protection you can give your true self is to become resilient to daily setbacks, and to learn flexible ways of moving around them so that your pleasure in your job is not only maintained but also enhanced.

This strengthening requires a whole-of-self approach. You may need to learn extra skills but, beyond that, on a daily basis you require physical vitality, mental flexibility and clarity, emotional resilience, and a commitment to experimenting with easier ways of doing things. You must also learn to trust your intuition and to have faith in the power and love that is inherent in your spiritual nature. These are the themes of the 10-Day Course.

Getting The Best Value From The Course

As described in How To Use This Book, you should choose to read the topics according to your sense of what resonates with you rather than proceeding in a sequential fashion over ten days. It is not even necessary to cover all the topics because some of these skills you may already use. Or, alternatively, you will not be drawn to them because your higher self knows you are not yet ready for those developments.

Several of the topics require you to set time aside on a free day to explore them, but the visualizations can be fitted into your schedule at the beginning or end of your day.

As the skills for making work Good need practice, at the end of each exercise you are given the opportunity to apply it more broadly in a Follow Through option. If you sense that a particular skill will strengthen you, exploring it more deeply is worth the effort.

Nevertheless, if you do not have the time or inclination for skill building, the practice of even a few techniques that you enjoy from time to time will yield results that are subtle but profound.

The Course is not designed for groups but you might like to consider sharing your experiences with a friend for extra insight and enjoyment.

Adjusting Your Brain To Experimentation

Making work activities fit your own design with only your true self to guide you is challenging both mentally and emotionally, especially in highly structured jobs or pressured workplaces. This is not, however, a reason to drop a plan to make your job more rewarding; minimal adjustments are always possible. However, this is not easy when rigid ways of approaching tasks dominate your thinking. Your brain needs to learn how to experiment, rather than following the known way.

The next visualization is designed to reduce the rigidity of a brain used to following structures and processes imposed by past conditioning. It encourages your brain to stretch beyond its comfort zone by looking for ways to make something you dislike or find unfamiliar more pleasant. It helps you stay open minded.

VISUALIZATION #14
Experimenting With Possibilities

The visualization has two stages. Stage 1 induces a state of relaxation by lifting you away from coalface concerns. This state is a necessary preparation for the right brain creativity of Stage 2. However, it is very pleasant to do as a stand-alone visualization.

In Stage 2, your brain is moved into creative mode. If you find this stage too demanding, practise Stage 1 only until you are drawn to try Stage 2 later.

There are many experimental possibilities in Stage 2, which can be overwhelming. Create just one pleasant food combination for each practice if you find this exercise is tiring. When your brain becomes adept at experimenting you can increase the complexity of your combinations.

As this visualization is a long process, we recommend you make a recording using your own voice. This recording will not be suitable for anyone else.

Stage 1

1. Go to your Inner Garden of Serenity and Well-Being (Visualization #1, How To Use This Book.)
2. Relax fully.
3. Walk from your garden into the countryside at night. Let the countryside be open. However, whether it is rolling or flat, high or low will depend on your sense of what you would most like.

4. The stars are shining brightly, very clear, and very high. There are no clouds.
5. A campfire is burning there, warm and glowing. Sit close to the fire. Let it warm your back and all parts of you that need it. Make it fun to be with this experience in any way that is right for you.
6. Then, still close to the fire's warmth, feel your awe and wonder of the night sky. Really feel it.
7. Become aware that the world is turning ever so slightly. A new dawn is below the horizon. Although you cannot see it you know it is there. But you feel no urgency that it should come quickly because you are enjoying the night sky so much.
8. Absorb the energies of wonder and pleasure fully.
9. If you wish to, continue to Stage 2.

Stage 2

1. Around the fire are four different plates and a sturdy cooking stick.
2. On these plates are different types of foods: two non-sweet foods, such as potatoes and whole tomatoes, and two sweet fruits, bananas and pears. You can choose any other non-sweet and sweet foods, including meat if that appeals, but all must be easily cooked on a stick. Your selection should include at least one item that seems difficult to combine.
3. Using your creative imagination, experiment with combining the four different foods to cook, taste and eat. (You will imagine that they all cook perfectly in a very short time.)
4. Have fun. Take your time. The more different foods you can combine, the better. As you eat, imagine the experience fully. Notice what you like and what you don't. When you

come across a combination that you do not like, play with the amount and combinations of food until you do like it.

5. If all the foods you choose are enjoyable in combination, take a note of what it is that makes it so.
6. When you have created a combination, relax by the fire and bring to mind your discoveries made through experimenting.
7. Rest now and enjoy the fire and the night sky.
8. A new dawn is below the horizon. Although you cannot see it you know it is there. But you feel no urgency that it should come quickly because you are enjoying this night of discovery so much.
9. Finish the visualization when you are ready to leave this experience.
10. Return to this visualization another day. Keep trying different food combinations until you are comfortable with doing this.

Follow Through Option: Experimenting In Real Life Activities

The visualization opens your brain to let you be more experimental in your approach to tasks. But this pathway must be used to become integrated. Therefore, after you are comfortable with Visualization #14, start to experiment with how you work in real life. Begin by choosing just one activity. Approach this in a relaxed and playful way because relaxation and playfulness fire up your right-brain creativity. Think of all the different ways you could change that activity to make it easier or more fun.

Remember that your aim is to learn your own unique ways to make the effort of work rewarding and relatively smooth.

DAY I

SELF-AWARENESS ON THE JOB

I don't like work–no man does–but I like what is in the work–the chance to find yourself. Your own reality–for yourself not for others–what no other man can ever know. They can only see the mere show, and never can tell what it really means.

Joseph Conrad

Self-awareness on the job is the springboard for turning work to your advantage. The habit of consciously observing and reflecting upon your experiences while you work has two benefits. It helps to identify exactly what processes you do enjoy, what types of media you prefer, and under what conditions you find a task dull, exhausting or frustrating. This information indicates the preferences of your true self. Any long-term choice you make will be the wiser for knowing these things.

However, the second benefit is more immediate. Self-awareness allows you to consider what present-time adjustments to your body, your attitude or the activity itself would promote what master psychologist, Abraham Maslow, referred to as flow: a state of energized focus that he believed only occurred when tasks met one's abilities.

Flow is much easier when you are using your natural strengths, but it never lasts and cannot be guaranteed because even one's talents involve activities that are not appealing. Furthermore, passion for any tasks expands and contracts naturally. However, clearing negativities as soon as practicable recovers flow faster, gives it longevity and makes obligatory tasks more tolerable.

It is likely that you have a habit of resigning yourself to emotional discomfort. If this is the case, your mind has to learn to take it seriously. Once you can observe the sources of anxieties and worries you can clear them quickly. Good Work depends on this! If you deny emotional negativities, they will come back to bite you in the form of things going wrong.

The self-awareness exercise below asks you to record the results of focused self-observation over several hours. It encourages the ability to live in the Now.

Here is an illustrative model. I have italicized my responses and insights.

Writing

I felt confused about what to write today. I came up with a few ideas that seem to answer the muddle but I know I am not there yet. I feel *frustrated* and *fearful about the lack of flow*. Power blackout stopped work for an hour. *Angry at having to switch focus* so shook out the irritation from my body. Actually *the interruption gave my mind time out* and when I got back to it, new ideas came in quickly.

House painting

It was patch-up time as the last step in repainting my study door. I fiddled about trying to fix minor blemishes. *I got angry as this kind of thing makes me feel overly contained and perfectionist*. I am not naturally good with my hands. However, *very pleased to see the final result* - door looks fresh and clean. *But next time someone else will be doing the painting*!

The garden

This was a clean-up effort. My partner mulched so it looked really good after my effort. It is *uplifting to be doing this with a companion* and it's a *lovely warm day. Fun for an hour only!*

Shopping

Didn't seem to think of it as work. I thought about what food I could buy that would be good in the hot weather but not too much bother to make. Not caring probably helped!

TECHNIQUE #8
Increasing Self-Awareness At Work

Stage 1

1. Choose a half-day for this project where you have a variety of jobs to do and plenty of time to think about what you are doing. Work at home is recommended.
2. For a minimum of two hours, observe yourself as you undertake all activities that are 'work', meaning that they require the conscious use of resources and effort to reach a certain outcome.
3. As you go, jot down the events and note your emotional and mental responses to each activity. It is important to record positive responses and discoveries as well as negative ones, as I have done in the template provided in the Notes to this chapter.
4. Take a break before moving to Stage 2.

Stage 2

Re-read and review your record. Ask yourself the following questions.

1. What situations/conditions/activities did I enjoy?
2. At what points did I feel engaged and in charge of my work?
3. What problems were truly beyond my control?
4. Which thoughts, decisions or behaviour helped me to create satisfaction in a particular activity?
5. Which single fear or worry about the situation or myself most reduced my enjoyment of the work?

Stage 3

Apply the following visualization to one identified fear. When we use the word fear we are referring to any inner state that does not promote a sense of well-being, comfort or pleasure. (In the template example I cleared the frustration about lack of flow in my writing.)

VISUALIZATION #15

The Jell-O Wall: Moving Beyond Anxiety And Worry

The Jell-O Wall visualization dissolves any anxiety, worry or negativity you are consciously aware of. However, its larger purpose is to break down the wall of unconscious fear and chronic resistance that continually interferes with your enjoyment of work and life itself.[1] Used over time, it lowers the tendency to respond to problems with knee jerk anxiety.

---

1 *The Jell-O Wall* visualization will not in itself relieve extreme conditions such as panic or obsessive anxiety. It will, however, complement other methods you find effective, including medication. If anxiety becomes chronic or extreme, consider professional assistance.

1. Close your eyes, relax your body and draw to mind the worry or fear identified in either the self-awareness exercise or one you know disturbs your normal work.
2. Create a clear picture in your mind of what your work would look and feel like if you did not have this concern.
3. Imagine standing in front of a high wall of Jell-O or gelatin in front of you. You notice it is made of large bricks.
4. You cannot see easily through the wall because the Jell-O is distorting the view to the positive future you would like to have. Pick a brick in the wall. Label it with the conscious fear you wish to release.
5. Place your hands on the brick. Make this experience a very sensory one: feel the cold, clammy, damp quality of the gelatin and the rubbery texture.
6. Now feel the warmth of your hands melting the Jell-O. You might like to imagine that the warmth contains a particular personal strength you have, such as clarity of mind, humor or generosity.
7. Gradually the warmth of your hands melts the brick so that you have a peephole to the clear future – though at first it may be a bit fuzzy! Take some time to sense this clear view even if you do not see it well.
8. Walk slowly and purposefully through the wall, feeling the gelatin sticking and then breaking easily away.
9. On the other side you find a natural pool of great purity and beauty. Brush off the residue of Jell-O that sticks to you. Jump into the pool, clearing the last stickiness away.
10. Climb from the pool, completely clean and refreshed.

11. Before finishing the visualization find a place to sit in the sunshine of your new, fearless environment. Experience this through your senses, in your mind, and in your heart. Feel the wonder and enjoyment. You are using this final step to create a picture of what you want your life to be, rather than just cleansing the anxiety.

Highly Recommended Extra Practice

Fear clearing is tedious because chronic fears are repetitive and addictive. They are like deep ruts in the brain, and as much as we would like to say that you will get rid of them in a day or even ten, you will not! You must practice the visualization regularly for it to be permanently effective. Fortunately, practicing *The Jell-O Wall* takes very little time: about one minute for each fear.

Remove individual bricks in the Jell-O wall when you become aware of anxieties and worries that come up each day. Examples: 'The boss is not going to like this' or 'Oh, no! Here comes that difficult customer again!'

Many people experience an appreciable drop in chronic levels of anxiety after four to eight weeks of intensive practice. If you choose to do this, it is important to choose different fears each day, rather than using the technique for the same anxiety over and over. To do so will only reinforce how 'difficult' the fear is. After your first month, practice staying aware of anxious twinges, and use it whenever concerns or worries arise.

DAY 2

THE RHYTHMS OF VITALITY

Age to me means nothing. I can't get old; I'm working. I was old when I was twenty-one and out of work. As long as you're working, you stay young. When I'm in front of an audience, all that love and vitality sweeps over me and I forget my age.

George Burns[1]

When work is tedious, excessive or emotionally draining it is always tiring. Good Work, on the other hand, brings vitality. It is life-giving at many levels.

But there is no doubt that even Good Work makes demands upon your energy resources and, at times, will stretch you beyond your limits. When your vitality is lowered, Good Work trickles away; the capacity to think clearly and creatively, or to handle emotional situations is impaired.

Therefore, a key to sustaining the positive attitude that is part and parcel of Good Work is making sure that your tasks do not diminish your vital energy to the point where you lose resilience.

---

1 http://www.arts-stew.com/classic-stars/actors-entertainers/george-burns-quotes-on-growing-old/

The ways a person maintains vitality are usually categorized under the headings of health and physical fitness. However, fitness does not prevent mental burnout or emotional overwhelm, nor does health alone ensure that you will remain a person who is truly enjoying the exercise of your spiritual gifts and talents; there is many an elderly person who has no desire to live to 100 simply because they know that having a body fit enough to survive is not enough to make life worthwhile.

Of course, appropriate physical exercise, fresh air, adequate nutrients and a diet that promotes energy are essential for vitality. But attending to the body is only part of the story; vitality is also created by feeding oneself pleasurable mental, emotional and spiritually uplifting experiences.

When you have work that provides all-round nourishment vitality is much easier to sustain. However, in those areas where your job does not support you, the reservoir of life energy can be filled through leisure activities that give pleasure in the ways that your job does not. This is particularly important if you are working 'just for the money'.

Vitality is also dependent on periods of total disengagement from every aspect of your life that involves effort, which is why holidays away from home are so rejuvenating. However, finding a significant amount of time out for complete disengagement is rarely possible. Because this is so, a working person must find ways to maintain vitality in a sustainable way every day.

Reflection

What do you currently do on a regular basis to maintain your vitality?

Learning To Sustain Vitality

One of the most pernicious effects of our relationship to machines is that people too often identify with them as benchmarks for personal capacity. If we are not on the go 24/7 as a machine can be, there is an underlying suspicion that something is amiss: we must be ill, weak, lazy, or over-55 (never a good thing). To some extent the Western world still believes in Rudyard Kipling's Victorian-era exhortation to fill the 'unforgiving minute' with activity, or risk being considered morally suspect.

However, the reality is that we are living beings whose personal output is subject to natural cycles, biological requirements and individual idiosyncrasies. The ability to work productively, and especially creatively, is dependent not on those engineering and design efficiencies that permit a machine to spew out product but on one's own unique rhythms being respected.

Because of the business world's mechanistic attitude to human nature you are likely to be unaware of your inner energy reserves until you are virtually running on empty. This common habit is one reason why people tend to rely on stimulants or their own nervous energy when extra energy is needed. They obtain a false, but ultimately harmful, sense of vitality in doing so.

Maintaining natural vitality is achieved by becoming aware of your personal rhythms of energy output and input so that you can adjust tasks to take account of them. Honoring these rhythms permits optimal productivity that is not robbing Peter to pay Paul. In practical terms this means that you can only do so much of a certain kind of work before you must change gear: tasks that require mental focus might be followed by physical exercise, a talk to a friend, or a bit of daydreaming. This way each part of the self is exercised and nourished rhythmically. The tide comes in and goes out, the seasons change, your life energy expands and retreats as it moves from one aspect of self to another.

By changing the nature of your activities you will find that your efficiency or productivity increases. Wasted time and mistakes due to stress will be reduced because each aspect of the self is given time to recuperate.

Technique #9 trains you to observe your vitality levels so that you can make adjustments to sustain self-care. It has to be done at home on a free day when you have domestic chores, but no other pressing obligations. If that is not possible in the near future, go immediately to Visualization #16, *Absorbing The Energies Of Vitality* that follows. Repeat that visualization several times before returning to the technique here another day.

TECHNIQUE #9
Observing The Rhythms Of Vitality

Workaholics tend to resist this exercise strongly on the grounds that it is wasting time that could be better spent on their obligatory tasks. If you are one of these, go first to Visualization #13, *Releasing Resistance And Procrastination*, Chapter 19.

Stage 1: Preparation

You need a minimum of three hours free time to observe your rhythms of vitality. Make arrangements so this can happen.

Prepare a list of domestic or self-care chores you would like to get done ahead of time.

Stage 2: Observing The Tides Of Vitality

1. When you wake in the morning, rate your sense of vitality from 1 – 5, 1 being the lowest score and 5 the highest. Make a mental note of this.
2. Stay in bed until your body tells you it wants to get up. (It doesn't matter if you don't get up until the three hours are over!) Rate your vitality again.
3. Now that you are ready to go, sense which of your chores is the one you feel most like doing: the one that promises

the greatest enjoyment. (This is likely to include self-care activities such as showering or eating breakfast but make sure that you genuinely want to do them. Don't just follow your normal routine on autopilot.)

4. As you go about the first activity, identify what part of yourself is being most used: physical, mental or emotional.
5. Stay alert for when that activity starts to become tedious or tiring, or when you zone out. This is the sign that your vitality is beginning to wane. You need to change the task even if it is not fully completed. You can come back to it later.
6. Each time you realize you should change activity, ask yourself what activity on your list of chores might now increase your vitality. This will often mean turning to a task that is markedly different from the earlier one, however, it can also mean that you need to take a short break, eat, take a walk in fresh air, or talk to someone. Don't judge that. Your aim for these three hours is to explore vitality, not to complete the to-do list.
7. At the end of the three-hour period, rate your vitality once again. If you have maintained your original rating or improved upon it, you have been able to work in ways that permit natural rhythm.
8. Ask yourself what you learned from this exercise and if you enjoyed this process or not.
9. If you did not, ask yourself what feelings, attitudes, or thoughts prevented you from enjoying it. These negativities need to be addressed and dissolved.

Example of a vitality report from one of our Siramarti Process students.

'Well, my greeting at 4.45 am was the dog deciding to vomit in our bedroom and hallway, so come Sunday morning when I woke my vitality levels were to say the least very low. So firstly I had to clear my anger. Then I cleared my fears, which made a significant difference, bringing almost excitement to doing the exercise.

The main things I noticed were:

I didn't complete most of the tasks on the list of chores.

Instead, I did other chores that weren't on the list e.g., re-cleaning the carpet from where the dog had been sick! I got vitality from this by cleaning other stains on the carpet that I had wanted to do for a long time...

I had to continually focus on vitality. It was not something that came naturally.

I needed to keep changing the type of chores I was doing to maintain vitality i.e. had to do something for me, then a household job.

To maintain vitality I had to notice my mind, my emotions and my body. My body was the one that felt the most discomfort when losing it.

I am looking forward to carrying out the exercise in the work place during the week.'

Later this woman reported that maintaining her vitality levels at work was much more difficult, but her increased awareness revealed her emotional tendency to become overly involved in projects that drained her. She began to disengage from these situations using Visualization #20, *Disentangling From The Energetic Impact Of Other People*, Day 7.

Using The Energy Of Feel-Good Experiences To Restore Vitality

Training your brain to accept the need for ease is part of learning how to main your vitality. If you connect to the energetic frequencies of pleasurable thoughts as often as possible, even for very short times, your anxiety about letting go of work obligations will reduce.

Feel-good thoughts trigger the hormones that promote the embodied sensation that life is a pleasure.

VISUALIZATION #16
Absorbing The Energies Of Vitality

As this visualization is quite long, it is best to memorize it in stages until you are confident.

Its effectiveness does not depend on the details of the image itself but how your body, rather than your mind, responds to it. You are recalling the energy of vitality that the image radiates to you. It does not matter whether the experience is in the present or the past. Simply calling up a feel-good image is sufficient.

1. Choose a place and time when you know you will not be interrupted to practice this visualization.
2. Ensure you are sitting in a warm, comfortable and protected environment.
3. Close your eyes and relax fully taking your mind consciously through each part of the body to let go of stored tension.
4. Imagine you are drawing the energy of the earth up through your body from your feet to your head and above.
5. Now draw down a ray of warm sunshine from above. Feel it touch the top of your head and let it flow fully down the body and enter the earth.
6. Imagine these two energies mingling in the centre of your chest and radiating into a cocoon around you.

7. Let the memory of a sight or scene that you associate with vitality come gently into your mind, for example, baby animals playing; spring bulbs shooting through the winter soil; a child laughing.
8. Take a few minutes to develop this scene fully and to ask yourself what it is about the image that gives you such a sense of vitality. Do not hurry this step.
9. Notice your body as it responds to the scene in your mind. Now focus on the body sensations and allow your body to accept them fully. Allow yourself to feel this vital life energy flowing through you.
10. Identify the main emotion you are experiencing. For example, wonder, serenity, bliss, excitement or confidence.
11. Place your hand over your heart and ask how you feel about your self at this moment.
12. Enjoy this feeling for as long as you wish before exiting the practice.

Follow Through Option: Staying Aware Of Your Vitality Levels During Normal Work

On one of your normal working days, observe the rhythms of your vitality throughout the day. Simply noticing that it is diminishing will be enough to encourage you to take a very short break, to stretch your body, or to reach for a glass of water. Avoid caffeine or smoking though! Remember you are looking for how you create natural vitality, not substance-induced support for it.

DAY 3

CLEAR AND PRESENT ACTION

More important than the quest for
certainty is the quest for clarity.[1]

Francois Gautier

In Chapter 9, Making Dreams Real, I described how to create a dream for one's working life that engages every aspect of the self. This dream is the starting point for actions that will take you to Good Work. However, some people find this process difficult partly because the very idea of having a personal dream for their job is strange and unsettling.

One man I coached, upon being asked to list his personal goals for his job, declared with real anger, 'Nobody, but nobody, ever does this! You just do what the boss says.' No strategy to make his work suit him better was possible because his Work-is-Sorrow victim mentality had led him to believe that having personal goals for work was a nonsense.

A dream or a purpose gives a reference point as to what actions are useful in getting to where you want to be. However, some people, especially

1 Francois Gautier. (n.d.). AZQuotes.com. Retrieved from AZQuotes.com Web site: http://www.azquotes.com/quote/767306

right brain orientated dreamers, often feel foggy and confused when faced with the question of where to start, even when they know the general direction they need to take.

Lack of mental clarity, and panic about it, can also bring on unwillingness to do anything at all for fear that nothing will guarantee a positive outcome. In this case, the mental focus falls on trying to dream up certainty rather than observing what is actually happening in order to find one practical exit out of the immediate muddle. This paralysis ends up in a cycle of self-negating, useless thoughts such as, 'What am I doing with my life? There I go again. Another wasted year in this job!' Genuine and deep spiritual weariness sets in.

The following visualization will relieve the fatigue that affects your capacity to be clear about the next step. Use it as required. If you do not wish to use it now, skip the visualization and continue reading.

VISUALIZATION #17
The Pool Of Renewed Vitality And Clarity

1. Find a quiet, comfortable and warm place where you will not be interrupted.
2. Close your eyes and relax your body from the toes up. Make sure your face, jaw, shoulders and hands are included in this process.
3. Imagine that you are transported to your Inner Garden of Serenity and Well-Being (Visualization #1, How To Use This

Book). Take some time to smell the fragrant natural scents, feel the temperature of the air and touch the earth or water.

4. Allow the place to grow even more beautiful. Sense how safe it feels.
5. Now walk through this place to find a pool of vitality. There is a sign indicating that you have found it. There are multi-colored, diamond-bright bubbles sparkling in it, as if it were a magical spa.
6. Step into the pool, naked. Feel the bubbles tickling your skin. Play with the vision and the joy of it. Allow the bubbly energy of vitality to be absorbed through your skin. Draw it fully into your bones and blood.
7. Take plenty of time to do this so that you truly do feel the energy of it in your body.
8. Let the colored bubbles turn to pure light. All around you is the pleasure and wonder of this vitality. Absorb this light into your body. Let it flow where it wishes to go.
9. Move out of the visualization when you feel complete.

Recovery From Inertia

When you find yourself in a bog of inaction it is best to stop worrying about your long-term future, which at that point will feel overwhelming. Instead start from the bottom up by looking at where you could experiment with small, precise improvements in the current situation.

The same advice applies to people who find dreaming for larger possibilities difficult. No matter whether you are a natural dreamer or not, taking one small action that turns around a negativity will automatically move you in the direction of Good Work.

But how will you find which action is best? To discover this requires a process of mental containment: you separate the problem into separate parts so that you can act with greater clarity. Begin by defining your task, your aim, and your chief immediate difficulty. Then create a series of logical actions that lead towards a solution of the difficulty.

Here is a personal illustration of the process of mental containment to solve a difficulty I had in writing Day 3: Clear and Present Action.

Overview of the problem

Today I am faced with writing a chapter about the importance of clear and present action to move work forward, but it is not coming easily to me. I have tried many different approaches and nothing is working to my satisfaction. I feel foggy and muddled. I need to gain clarity.

My task

Writing about the importance of Clear and Present Action.

Work out my main aim/purpose/dream

To provide useful information that demonstrates the key principles of containment in as clear a way as possible.

Apply whole self-awareness to my experience of the problem

I am *most aware* of my mental state. I am mentally overwhelmed because there are so many pieces of information that might be relevant to discussing containment. I observe my emotional state: the mental confusion is creating anxiety and frustration. I notice my physical state: I feel slightly headachy.

Identify the most pressing problem

To reduce the mental overwhelm.

Think up possible actions to solve this problem

I brainstorm the possible ways to solve the mental overwhelm by: a. creating some kind of order in my thinking by writing my thoughts out; b. draw up a mind map to work out priorities; c. take a breather by doing something else; d. talk to someone to get their ideas.

Decide which of the choices feels best

I choose the quickest and most appealing method as my first experiment in solving the problem. I write out what I am doing and how I am thinking and feeling step-by-step.

Evaluate the effect of the action

Fortunately, my choice of experimental action proves effective immediately. The benefits of writing an analysis of the problem prove to be three-fold.

First, I feel calmer and clearer because I find a way to put some kind of order into the problem.

Second, in choosing to write rather than using the other options I also uncovered a simple strategy that illustrates one way to become mentally clear that readers might find useful. In short, I have also moved towards the aim I set myself for the task.

Finally, reflecting on this process gives me a clue to a larger dream. By amplifying my aim for the day's writing I can see that having *many* readers finding the whole book useful to their mental clarity is something I really want.

The process of containment will not guarantee that you find the answer to Life, the Universe and All That, but addressing the problem in a broad but contained way is half the battle to moving in the right direction. In particular, it stops you feeling emotionally overwhelmed because progress is assured.

TECHNIQUE #10
The One Step Forward From a Difficult Present

Clarity is primarily a mental ability. However, one's capacity for focus is strongly influenced by one's feeling state. If you become emotionally distracted, then problem solving becomes difficult. For this reason, gaining clarity often begins with identifying and clearing the emotional or mental disturbance that affects one's ability to think clearly. The following process will help you to work out the most important emotional or mental blockage that needs to be cleared.

1. Using your current work (paid or unpaid) as your database, write a description of a single process that you are currently engaged in. For example, if you are making a video, you might focus only on sourcing props for it. Make notes of all your responses to that activity, both positive and negative.
2. To become clear about what disturbance you want to change, flip the most pressing negative to find a present aim. Example: 'This job is physically overwhelming' points to a clear goal to reduce the physical demands on you.
3. Now think up as many ways as you can to achieve this goal. Don't be practical at this point because that will stop your creative right brain hemisphere working for you.
4. Choose to act on just one of those ideas. This must be the one that your left-brain feels is the most easy and painless.
5. Evaluate the effects of your action.
6. If the result is not satisfactory, choose another method from

your brainstorm list. Continue experimenting until you feel more positive, even in the smallest way.

Follow Through Option

If you wish to apply the process of containment to improving employment in a very toxic workplace, the overwhelming nature of the discomfort may tempt you to throw the whole job in rather than bothering to analyze it.

However, learning to change a broad problem bit-by-bit is more empowering in the long run than changing a job immediately. You are developing a skill that can be taken anywhere in the future, and one you will always find useful.

Begin by deciding which one of the problems is giving you the most emotional grief. Use the One Step process to address that issue. The relief of a small change may make the job tolerable or help you to see opportunities within it.

The Power Of Making A Small Change: Steve C's Story

Steve was new to his somewhat chaotic and stressful workplace. He found it overwhelming at many levels and thought there was nothing he could do to improve the situation. He wanted to leave to find a 'better' position although he had no idea what that might look like: he had no bigger picture dream. As resentment was feeding his sense of overwhelm, I suggested that he take the single step of focusing on only the positive aspects of his job for several weeks.

'Hi Suzie,

I just wanted to let you know the result of taking the one step of looking for positives at work.

At first all I could think of was stuff like sitting in my car at lunchtime with the radio on, away from work and also the taste of my lunch. But gradually my eyes began to open and I saw a whole lot of things that were positive in the workplace itself. For example, I had a wonderful chat with a regular customer that really uplifted me. I had the most gorgeous child smile at me. A colleague bought me a chocolate out of the blue. Suddenly a new staffer came on board who helped with the overload!

I was amazed. After a couple of weeks of doing this I came up with a long list of positive experiences at work. I gradually changed my entire perspective. I have stopped looking for a new job. I feel really fortunate to have the one I have.'

Reflection

This worker took one step to relieve his negative thinking, which worked well. However, his report has more gems to be discovered. What do his illustrations of the positives he found indicate about the nature of this student's true self (Chapter 16) and the kind of future work he would likely enjoy?

DAY 4

SHINING YOUR LIGHT

Our deepest fear is not that we are inadequate. Our deepest fear is that we are powerful beyond measure. It is our Light, not our Darkness, that most frightens us. We ask ourselves, who am I to be brilliant, talented, gorgeous, fabulous? Actually, who are you NOT to be?

Marianne Williamson

In Chapters 6 and 16 you were introduced to the nature of the true self's powers. These powers hold both light (intuitive insights relevant to your projects), and love (the ability to create well-being, enjoyment, ease or fun). In combination, light and love make your projects glow.

Regrettably, we often fear accepting our powers despite the fact that the greatest satisfaction comes from using them. This is true even for many individuals who like their job, and are respected for it. Such people will often settle for their work beingery good but not inspirational. They do not dare to acknowledge that it is worthy of being elevated to spiritual uniqueness.

However, whenever you shy away from a true self power, you are depriving yourself of the conditions in which it can grow: you will not explore it, invest in it or make a stand for it. And, in the long run, you will feel disappointed that you have let yourself down through resisting it.

The reasons for this resistance vary from person to person, but they all boil down to a fundamental attitude that one is not sufficiently capable or deserving of the right to express the full power of one's potential. Nevertheless, overcoming this fear is essential because the difference between work that is good enough and Good Work lies in its creator having confidence in its radiance; in short, in knowing that no one else can sing like you do: and for that reason the world needs your song.

Strengthening Your True Self's Powers

Even when you are willing to accept your true self's powers, they need strengthening to make them shine, and this takes effort and resources. The usual way of refining Good Work is to focus on overcoming one's limitations rather than polishing the strengths. This approach is, for other than basic requirements, an inefficient (and frustrating) use of time.

Think of a small business owner who has problems with written expression trying to copy-write advertisements for his company. He will make far better use of his time by indulging his genuine interest in sales trends through enrolling in a marketing course or designing his own customer survey. His new knowledge is fun to acquire, and can also feed into his assessment of whether a paid copywriter is speaking to his market. A natural synergy occurs as the information derived from his passion and the copywriter's skill combine to optimize his business. His marketing effort can shine in a way that it never could if he had struggled to master his limitation.

Reflection

Take five minutes to remember a moment when you were feeling at ease with an activity. Recall the skill you were using *and* the personality strength that gave radiance to the task, such as attention to detail, relaxation, curiosity or passion for the material you were using. The shining light you gave that task came from you, not from exercise of the skill alone.

If struggling with limitation does not help your true self to shine through your work, what does? The brief answer is to seek anything at all that makes *you* feel lighter: to clear negativities, to stay relaxed and humorous, to make processes as easy as possible, to get extra help when you need it, and to increase your competencies in those skills that support your talents.

However, because these methods are very much of this world, also give yourself occasional time out to reconnect with your spiritual core so that you can bask in its frequencies, and in that way have a more intimate knowledge of the energies that underpin your true self. The next inner journey shows you one way of doing this.

The Glory Of Your Spiritual Core

So often in life we focus on the mundane or the miserable. In making your work Good your attention turns more and more towards the natural aptitudes you have and the positive emotional rewards that working with them brings. But this shift of focus is awkward because the adult brain is geared towards coping with the struggles that earning a living entails.

A child has natural optimism and passion born out of its unimpeded access to its true self, but by the time it reaches maturity much of that has been put aside. The next uplifting inner journey helps you to reconnect with the true self's energy. It is effective because whatever energy in Nature deeply attracts us reflects an aspect of our core spirit's natural qualities.

When you repeat it, the scene may vary. Allow this to be; your magnificence is a multi-faceted jewel.

VISUALIZATION #18
Experiencing The Magnificence Of Your True Self's Energy

1. Close your eyes. Relax a moment.
2. Draw to mind a place of awesome natural beauty, a place from memory such as a glowing sunset seen from a beach, a mighty mountain, a quiet and fertile valley, or a majestic waterfall. Use all your senses to recall the experience. Immerse yourself in the beauty. Feel and see it all around you.
3. Bring your attention to your heart. Imagine that you are breathing the feelings that this awesome beauty inspires in you into your heart: the sense of wonder, serenity, power or ageless beauty.
4. Keep breathing, filling your whole body with this magnificence until you are so full that it gently radiates out from you to a comfortable distance.
5. Imagine you can now see yourself glowing inside this magnificent beauty. You may like to imagine yourself stepping into it.
6. Sense how the energy of your radiant beauty and the radiance of this beautiful place connect in easy synergy. You are as one.
7. Know and feel yourself as the magnificent awe-inspiring being that you are.

Follow Through Option

Over the next 24 hours identify a power you have. Examples: your love of woodworking, your ability to play with children, a knack for finding useful information quickly. Sense how the energy of your engagement with these things adds glow to your life. When you are in these moments your true self is radiating its beauty into the world and warming, inspiring or soothing those you come in contact with.

How will you know when your work is shining? Answer: You will feel calm, confident and secure even when you are facing difficulties. You will be quietly proud of even small achievements and celebrate them frequently. People will value your work, talk about it, and recommend it.

DAY 5

EMOTIONAL RESILIENCE

I don't want to be at the mercy of my emotions.
I want to use them, to enjoy them....

Oscar Wilde

Practical restrictions, significant though they may be, are not the most important source of one's work feeling uncomfortable. Far more potent is the frustration or emotional vulnerability created by inefficient technical systems or a peevish boss.

The exercise of natural gifts is always a pleasure, but the continual need to adjust to factors beyond one's control triggers anger, anxiety and self-doubt. When frustration is intensified by the difficult reactions of others, these responses easily solidify into stress, resentment and withdrawal or, in the worst-case scenarios, hopelessness or paranoia.

Not knowing how to relieve uncomfortable emotions has a cumulative effect. Your attitude slowly becomes soured. No matter how talented and dedicated you are, a pall of negative energy surrounds you. This infects the very work itself, and other people's experience of it; they pick up on your loss of enthusiasm or barely suppressed anger. Therefore, boosting your emotional resilience is crucial to grow and sustain Good Work both before and after it is set in place.

Developing Emotional Savvy

Unfortunately most people have little emotional education to help them deal with negativity. Since Victorian times, powerful emotional reactions have generally been considered the embarrassing effect of being weak in some way: sad, bad, mad – and/or female. Admitting to such emotions is to admit vulnerability.

However, emotional energy is the key driver in human affairs and lacking knowledge of how it works and how to harness it appropriately is to deprive yourself of much happiness and personal power. The more you can learn how to embrace and harness your emotions, the more in charge of life you will feel. It is a twenty-first century life skill that everyone needs.

Two Different Responses To Emotional Difficulties

The key emotional discomforts that affect working relationships are anger, and fear or anxiety.

People handle these disturbances differently according to their preference for using the right or left hemisphere of the brain. Right brain orientated Sky types tend to withdraw from those who they perceive are the source of their problems. They focus on the technicalities of the task and deny others' perspectives – or they explode in pent-up frustration. Feeling powerless to handle the emotional storms of life, they develop a victim mentality in which others are always to blame for their misery.

Left-brain orientated Earth individuals avoid expressing those emotions that will rock the boat of social harmony. They repress any direct expression of bad feelings. However, gradually they develop an underlying resentment, which can be felt as a heavy and joyless attitude to work. Their work is an obligation, not a spark of soul. They become martyrs who whine silently (except to their best friends where pity parties abound) about how others are so uncooperative.

Both types hoard negativity that becomes the air they breathe, and it is for this reason that there is so much stress in so many workplaces.

Handling The Emotional Discomfort Of Anger And Anxiety

The skill of relieving both anger and anxiety involves a three-step process that does not immunize you against these natural human responses – even your true self needs them to guide you towards making work better – but instead gives strategies for being in charge of them.

Knowing how to ease your feelings quickly brings a speedy recovery from distress so that you can address the practical issues more constructively. You also gain greater self-confidence because you truly have more power to cope with the emotional rub of daily interactions.

I recommend you read the next information with a recent interpersonal experience at work in mind.

Step 1: Owning One's Emotions Fully

The first step in increasing emotional resilience is counterintuitive; it involves fully accepting one's emotions, not fighting or downplaying them. Focusing on a churning stomach or clenched jaw helps to identify the underlying emotion and admit the truth of it. This is far better than arguing it away. Just because your emotion may not seem 'reasonable' is no reason for disrespecting it. To override it is to invite stress, more problems, and ultimately ill health. It must be accepted for what it is: without judgment.

Paradoxically, however, your response to the situation is yours alone; it is not a truth necessarily shared by anyone else. Imagine your beloved dog is run over in the street; you will be grief-stricken. However, your neighbor who disliked your dog's barking may well be grateful for this event. Your grief is your own truth, but it does not alleviate the pain to accuse your neighbor of being a hard-hearted dog-hater. Their relief at the death of your dog is as valid an emotional truth as yours. And pointing the finger will not dissolve your distress; that is something you have to clear within yourself. No one else can do it for you.

Emotional resilience, therefore, starts with taking personal responsibility for owing the emotion, sensing its full impact, and accepting it as yours and yours alone to handle.

Step 2: Releasing Uncomfortable Energy

Although it serves no purpose to blame someone for causing your anger, when a person upsets you, there is often a valid practical point to be made. Someone has done something that needs to be addressed. You want to be sure that you will not be disturbed by their behavior in the future: the practical problem, separated from the emotional reaction you had to it, has to be sorted out.

However, an objection cannot be properly heard unless you first *release* the energy that envelops it. This must be done safely and privately. Intense emotional energy alarms other people and if you dump it, whether that is anxiety or anger, they will react accordingly. You will no longer be in charge of the situation because the other parties' feelings about *your* feelings will now be part of it. You are likely to end up in head-butting arguments or in a soup of manipulation and mistrust.

The *safe* release of emotional discomfort, using the techniques in this book or any other effective means, allows the mind and body to relax sufficiently for healing to occur. Letting go of the *energies* of anger, anxiety, hurt, outrage or panic calms the troubled waters of the mind so that practical wisdom can assert itself in resolving the practicalities. It also helps the other person to hear your objection because it is not wrapped in the force of frightening or repellent energy.

Whatever you do, don't jump into fix-it mode without identifying the emotions underpinning difficulties. This mistake is, unfortunately, disastrously common. It is the reason why so many apparently clever solutions to human issues prove mysteriously ineffectual. They appear logical but if they do not take account of emotional implications they soon come undone.

Step 3: Communicating The Problem

Done correctly, Steps 1 and 2 are remarkably effective in making you feel better. However, they do not replace skills in delivering any objection you have and negotiating win/win outcomes. We recommend training in communication and/or negotiation skills to in order to maintain your confidence in being able to resolve conflict.[1] Nevertheless, it is important to understand that even the most skillful interpersonal communication does not replace the need for energy release first; this is an essential preparation. The release phase must be genuine; if you pretend you are calm when you are not, your attempts to sort out hot issues will rest on wobbly energetic foundations.

The Importance Of Clearing Anger

Of all the negative emotions, anger has the greatest destructive impact on cooperative working relationships. It causes co-workers to recoil and it leads to fear, secretiveness and mistrust in subordinates. For some individuals, any expression of anger is experienced as abusive and terrifying, even if the issue is quite minor. They will shut down completely.

Unlike most other uncomfortable emotions, anger cannot be released

---

1 Nonviolent Communication (NVC), developed in the 1960s by Marshall Rosenberg, is one well-known form of such training.

through inner work alone. The physical body needs to be involved: shaking out the sensations, dancing, stamping, or chopping wood. Any vigorous body technique will be effective so long as it is done with the intention of releasing anger safely. Whichever technique you choose, keep your focus on where you feel the angry sensations in the body as you expel the energy. *Do not* continue the activity after the angry sensations have gone.

Immediate physical release, such as shaking out irritation, will relieve minor and passing annoyance. However, the Anger Letter below is best for unresolved or chronic relationship problems.

Writing out your anger is also the most useful form of release if you want to communicate your objections later.

Important! *Don't ever send an anger letter!* Always handwrite your letter and destroy it afterwards.

TECHNIQUE #11
The Anger Letter

1. For this technique[2], choose a colleague or boss where frustration or irritation has been a chronic experience. If you are angry with a whole crowd of people, identify the one you are most annoyed with, or who is representative of the group.
2. Handwrite a letter to a person you are in conflict with. In your letter express all the things you would like to say but don't.
3. Include the precise facts of how, when and why you are

[2] This technique has been adapted from one published in the Lazaris Material at www.lazaris.com. See Acknowledgments.

angry as well as where you have been angered by their behaviour in the past. This precision is important.

4. Write rapidly without pausing until you are done. Ignore correct spelling and punctuation. Write colorfully. Let obscenities come out if they want to.
5. While you are writing, stay aware of body tensions. Make a note of these as you write: Example, 'When I think of how you… my jaw tightens and my stomach is in knots. I feel like punching you.' This is an important step.
6. When you have completed the letter, put it aside in a secure place preferably overnight, or for at least four hours.
7. Read it over. Highlight the words and phrases that still have energy for you. Add extra details if necessary.
8. Once you have completed the process to this point, read your letter to find just one central practical problem. For example, that person changes policy without telling you so you often act on outdated information.
9. Now destroy the letter, preferably by burning it – very safely! If this is not possible, tear it up and flush it down the toilet.

You are now energetically ready to discuss the practical problem with the person concerned. However, if you choose to do this, make sure you prepare for this communication carefully so that the person is ready to hear you. Even when you have little anger left, your objection may cause them to react emotionally themselves.

Some Answers To Common Questions

Q. How do I know my anger has really been released?

A. If you are unsure that your anger has released, try writing an anger letter to the same person three or four days later. You will find that by releasing the energy in the first letter, there is little you want to say at the second attempt. If the anger remains it is likely that you have a reason for wanting to hoard it. You will need to explore why this is so, or seek professional counseling if you find that difficult. A chronic inability to release anger is likely to have deeper issues attached.

Q. I found I had a lot more than one practical problem with one of my colleagues. But your advice indicates that I can only communicate one of them. What do I do about the others?

A. People can absorb one or two messages at a time. This is the reason for the advice to communicate just one practical objection per meeting. If you have further problems, they need to be addressed later. That way you will not overload the other person emotionally, causing more trouble for yourself.

Q. I have done this technique several times and it does make me feel better, but I still find myself getting angry. What am I doing wrong?

A. Anger release techniques will not eradicate anger forever: anger is part of life. Sadly, people will go on irritating you! However, if you regularly take charge of it, it will not destroy your working relationships or undermine your Good Work enthusiasm.

Q. I use the anger techniques and find them quite effective. But there is one colleague who does not let up on his abusive behaviour. My anger letters seem to make no difference.

A. Anger release techniques will also not work well on those folk who feel that anger is the only strength they have to enforce their power or protect themselves. In these cases, a person needs to develop personal strength in others ways.

It will also fail to impress those who enjoy being aggressive. Aggression is not the same as anger. Physical protection from such people is required. If you find yourself in a situation where you are on the end of aggressive behaviour, it is time to get out of the situation.

Follow Through Option

This technique is wonderful for *all* conflict situations. Consider using it for other long-term interpersonal difficulties, including unresolved conflict with people that have hurt or disappointed you in the past.

DAY 6

SUSTAINABLE ENJOYMENT

The joy of life consists in the exercise of one's energies, continual growth, constant change, the enjoyment of every new experience... The eternal mistake of mankind is to set up an attainable ideal.

Aleister Crowley

Today's exploration assumes that you already have work that you genuinely enjoy. (If you do not have a job you like, you may prefer reading Part 6, Yes Buts..., Objection 5.)

Once you are in the position of having your true self engaged in at least one form of potential Good Work[1], you are on track for a spiritually fulfilling life that satisfies the dreams and ambitions you have for your work.

Unfortunately, this delightful situation can go unexpectedly pear-shaped if you lose balance between your commitment to your job and your

1 Although conventional thinking prefers to believe that Good Work should be found in a paid and preferably full time career, from the point of view of your true self this is false. So long as you can transform any kind of work into Good Work experiences, you have an avenue for spiritual growth and fulfillment as well as a means of contributing the best of your self to others.

willingness to find joy in the rest of your time on earth. If your participation in life congeals around the activities associated with it, you become a workaholic. Any change in direction, including holidays or short breaks, is resisted as straying from the path of your destiny. You justify the fact you haven't 'got a life' by all sorts of excuses. Your beloved job then deprives your true self of its need for multidimensional nourishment.

One of the main, but subtle, reasons for this problem is that the pleasure of Good Work can become addictive because of its stimulation factor. The stimulation of your talents and passions is, of course, a core reason for attachment to a job. Unfortunately this commitment can easily metamorphose into an adrenalin-fuelled obsessiveness, and gradually the ease in the work diminishes. Inevitably, your work becomes less Good.

The inner self-saboteur will often say that the pressure you now experience is because you are not achieving your goals fast enough. This same saboteur will turn to the socially approved remedies: just work harder or longer in order to reach the ticker tape faster. Of course, this is just a story but the tighter you hold to it, the more your discomfort will spread. As creeping fatigue sets in, creativity dissolves into a fog. Struggle takes over. Mistakes are made, possibilities overlooked. Important relationships go by the board.

By this stage Good Work is a tepid version of its original strength. However, you keep telling yourself that all is well, even though the job has lost its ability to support or grow you as a whole person. It has become a prison with bars that are invisible because you don't want to see them. And, unconsciously, you become frightened of life outside the prison because it is increasingly unfamiliar. Equally significantly, if this denial becomes chronic, the creative aspect of Good Work deteriorates. Work-is-Sorrow mentality returns with a vengeance.

Self-aware people usually recognize that things have to change before disaster strikes, but changing focus is naturally difficult if you have no other place for your mind to go other than your work. Your thoughts will keep returning to your projects, even though you would rather forget them. The wheel keeps spinning but the hamster is dead.

Reflection

Referring to the Wheel of Life in Chapter 8, assess with brutal honesty the degree of pleasure you are deriving from each sector by rating it from 0 - 5, where 0 is none and 5 is high.

Rate again, but this time in terms of how much attention you are giving to creating enjoyment in each sector.

Does this exercise suggest that you need to change your focus from work to other areas of your life for greater self-nourishment?

Raising The Hamster From The Dead

Unbalanced focus on work that rests on your spiritual gifts is an addiction. Addictions begin with the enjoyment they provide; they spiral into self-abuse.

However, holistic self-nourishment is a key true self need, and mandatory for Good Work. Therefore, if you are a workaholic, you must wean your mind off work by committing to other forms of pleasure until they provide an alternative. Unfortunately, attempts to recover whole self balance in this way will be hard to do because the enjoyment of the alternative activity will, initially, seem pale in comparison with the joy of being in the zone of Good Work.

What is worse, the inner saboteur will also whisper that you should keep soldiering on until one day you will have opportunities for more freedom. (Take no notice of it!)

In choosing a work substitute, look for those activities that promote relaxation, lightening up, or laughter. These will provide an antidote to the seduction of workaholism. Your resurrected hamster will begin to roll the Wheel of Life joyfully once again.

Holidays Without A Holiday

Apart from overwork and addictive attitudes, people often lose enjoyment of work if they are burdened by a sense of over-containment. This usually occurs when a project involves too many mandatory but personally meaningless activities, or ones that require close attention to tasks you are not particularly good at. During such times, even Good Work becomes heavy and claustrophobic.

The following visualization will help to inject a sense of freedom into your life whatever the cause of your loss of enjoyment. However, it does not replace the need to keep truthfully monitoring and addressing any symptoms of workaholism.

Reconnecting With Holiday Energies At Work

The delights of annual holidays are usually forgotten within a week back at work. This occurs because the brain compartmentalizes the expansive energies associated with holidays – freedom, ease, spontaneity, novelty, and relaxation – from the Work-is-Sorrow experiences of limitation, debilitating effort and routine. The regular injection of holiday energies into your day maintains the vitality required for Good Work.

Here is a report on doing so from one student who works in a public library.

'Today I decided to look at freedom at work.

I looked at creating freedom today - as opposed to how much freedom I generally have in this job. On Friday I work 10.30 am - 6.15 pm. I usually have to go to lunch at 1 pm. But today I asked the boss if I could go at 2 o'clock. This meant that after lunch I had a shorter day so time didn't drag as much as if I had lunch earlier.

Throughout the day I kind of just did what I liked, that is, I moved from returns, to customer service, to shelving, to doing the stationery order, to looking at technology on iPads without too much restriction. Generally I tend to do it all at once, that is, customer service is the first priority and I do everything else in between.

These changes helped me to create freedom. Although I certainly didn't feel like going to work in the morning - once I got there I didn't feel trapped in any way.'

VISUALIZATION #19
Absorbing Holiday Energies

This visualization is very straightforward, but before you practice it make a point of recalling the kinds of positive experiences you associate with holidays. People enjoy different kinds of experience from their holidays so it is necessary to identify those which most appeal to you.

1. Find a comfortable place, close your eyes, and relax.
2. Imagine you have now been transported to your favorite holiday destination. Step into the location fully, using all your senses.
3. Recall how you felt physically. Remember the particular emotional pleasure and the uplifting mental experiences. Allow the higher self to be brought forward by recalling the gut feelings and insights you experienced. Hold your whole-of-self enjoyment of this environment for as long as you can.

4. Focus on breathing in the energies of this holiday until your body responds to the memory.
5. Now come back to the present time, feeling revived.
6. Repeat this visualization regularly until you experience the positive feelings in the body easily.

Follow Through Option

Using the student example above as a guideline, choose one of your preferred holiday energies, such as freedom or relaxation, to seek out or create on a normal working day.

DAY 7

FREEDOM FROM OTHER PEOPLE'S IMPACT

To be nobody but yourself in a world which is doing its best,
night and day, to make you everybody else means to fight the
hardest battle which any human being can fight;
and never stop fighting.

e.e. Cummings

Human beings have two paradoxical needs: the urge to unite with others, and the desire to be respected for, and supported in, one's separateness. There is a great tension between these forces, which needs to be resolved if the Good Work of the true self is to flourish; you have to discover how to support your individuality while also cooperating comfortably with others.

The urge to belong is inbuilt. It is very powerful because being a member of a supportive family or group provides physical and material security, companionship, and the benefits of moral and emotional backup. However, the true self stands alone in its own perspectives and strengths. If the spiritual identity underpinning your work is to be expressed in its authenticity, it has to be freed from the force of those group energies, *whether positive or negative*, that are alien to it.

Without this protection your spirit's contribution will gradually be diminished to fit into the envelope of group expectations. Your work will be deprived of its uniqueness and can never be Good in the fullest sense. People who lose commitment to their true selves, either through fear, laziness or guilt, bow down to the theory that 'the boss/customer/balance sheet is always right.' They have given their spiritual power away to the collective.

Your natural aptitudes, personal qualities or service may not seem especially outstanding to you, but their value is far greater than you know. Consider the difference between food churned out by factories and those homemade meals prepared with the love and care inherent in a Good cook. The nutritional value may be the same but the experience is incomparable: the former keeps the body alive; the latter brings delight, appreciation and psychological comfort as well.

The abandoning of one's true self has broader implications because it is the creative potential held within an individual's special insights or different way of proceeding that so often leads a community out of the stagnation of the status quo into a land far richer than the collective mind can imagine.

Protecting the freedom of your true self, therefore, matters not only to your own well-being but also to the health of the world that needs its service. Once you are able to protect the true self in a gentle and effective way, you can operate with others on a win/win basis because your real needs and perspectives are brought to the table as part of a common effort.

Safeguarding The True Self

Protection from the undue influence of others has two aspects: first, the employment of *conscious strategies* to support your position, perspective or needs; and, second, the regular use of *energetic techniques* that safeguard against the invisible effects of group morale or forceful individuals.

Conscious Protection

There are a number of things you can do to protect yourself consciously from the temptation to give your power away. Most of these forms of protection are well understood. They are outlined here as reminders.

Mental protection

Mental protection involves taking the time to gather information or evidence, to support your position in an unbiased way. The aim of doing this is not to prove you are 'right' but to ensure that your viewpoint is respected and taken into account in any practical matters. Any logical step that makes your work easier or more effective is a means of giving the true self protection.

Emotional protection

Emotional protection begins with making certain that you do not hold emotional contaminants that will invite attack or manipulation. In other words, it is your responsibility to clear your own fears about other people (Visualization #15, Day 1) and your irritability (Technique #11, Day 5). Once you are in the habit of dropping the emotional burdens of worry, anxiety, anger and guilt, then your interaction with others will be far less charged, and in this way you will have greater influence.

Owing to the fact that negativity is so heavy and pervasive, it is also important to lift out of pessimism and naysaying by allowing yourself to feel the positives of your workplace, and the people in it.

Physical protection

There are times when no matter how skillful you are at proactively protecting yourself, the impact of others' negative behaviour or distress will be too great to handle. In these cases, removing yourself, even temporarily, from the possibility of abusive interactions is the only solution. Take care to ignore the self-destructive voice that tells you that it is weak or unnecessary to get help to do so. Your true self is valuable and as it is housed in your physical body that too must be protected.

Reflection

Which of the forms of conscious protection listed do you use to support yourself?

Protection From The Mysterious Power Of Energetic Influence

Even when you apply the conscious methods of protection, you will not necessarily be safe from the negative *energy* of others. Of all the forms of protection this is the least understood and, therefore, the most ignored; however, it is equally important to prevent yourself from being at the mercy of others.

People interact with one another energetically. We live in a sea of collective thoughts and feelings washing out in waves from those around us. We naturally absorb those frequencies, both uplifting and debilitating, as if they were our own. This may seem questionable to some readers but there is now a solid body of research that supports this assertion.[1] In other words, group feelings are infectious. You owe it to your true self and your Good Work to insulate yourself from the undue influence of others.

Reflection

Do people in your workplace feel reasonably safe and respected? If not, what negative attitudes do they hold in common? How do these attitudes subtly affect you?

---

1 https://www.psychologytoday.com/blog/high-octane-women/201210/emotions-are-contagious-choose-your-company-wisely

VISUALIZATION #20
Disentangling From The Energetic Impact Of Other People

The following key visualization is designed to protect you from the effects of poor workplace morale and individuals with whom you are in conflict. It will also alleviate the undue influence of people you respect. In short, it helps you to maintain your true self's integrity. You will not necessarily feel a strong emotional effect when you practice it, but you will observe yourself slowly feeling stronger in interactions with them.

Use it immediately you feel you are being influenced by a particular group, individual, or social situation. Use it also when you are worrying about another person's welfare, applying it to those with whom you have a positive relationship as well as to difficult people.

Whatever you do, practice it regularly with active focus and intention. Don't let it become a meaningless ritual. It won't work unless you are making a genuine choice to change the relationship dynamic.

Stage 1: Anchoring The Light

1. Relax. Close your eyes and breathe gently. Imagine you are standing on a green lawn or field.
2. Draw a circle in the grass at a comfortable distance from you. This is your personal space, your circle of power.
3. Now imagine that you are bending down and pulling energy from the earth up your body. Do this slowly and pretend

you can feel it rising up your legs, through your trunk, into your arms and up to your head.

4. Now look up and sense a warm ray of sunshine flowing over you and down into the earth. Again make this as real as possible in your imagination.
5. Visualize the two flows of energy moving up and down the spine.
6. Cross your hands over the centre of your chest. Imagine the energies are mingling there and radiating through your heart chakra until they form a cocoon of glowing, warm energy around you.

Stage 2: Disentangling

1. Outside your circle of power, sense the person (or group of people) from whom you wish to disentangle. It is not important to actually 'see' them.
2. Take your attention to your own energy field. Imagine that your energy has floated away from your circle of power to mingle with others. You may see this energy as strings attaching to particular individuals.
3. Make a clear choice that you no longer want to relate to people in this way.
4. Focus on the breath. On the in-breath, begin to firmly pull this energy back to you. Pull or suck the energy back into your centre. Allow it to travel down and anchor in the earth.
5. Imagine that some of your energy has glued itself to others so that, in bringing back your own energy, you have inadvertently pulled in others' energies as well. This energy is interfering with your own true responses even when that energy seems positive. Release this 'other' energy by gently

blowing it away or by expelling it through the pores of the skin and ends of the fingers and toes.

Stage 3: Sending Love

1. Once you feel the disentangling is completed, draw a ball of pure light and love from your heart to indicate your desire to bring well-being to the other as well as yourself. (This step is extremely important; if you do not do it the other party will begin to feel rejected or isolated, which will cause them to react.)
2. Throw this ball over the person or situation with which you have been entangled. It assists if you imagine this person or people inside a large glass container such as an aquarium that holds their energy from escaping.
3. Sense your ball of love light flowing over them and being absorbed into their own energy field so that they can move forward in relationship to you with respect and comfort.
4. Complete the exercise by imagining that you throw a transparent but impermeable bubble around your energy field to protect it from invasion throughout the day.

Follow Through Option

For five working days, choose just one person with whom you have difficulty to practice the disentangling exercise. Don't choose someone who is excessively aggressive as her or his energy is likely to be too strong for a beginner.

Begin by rating your sense of discomfort in the relationship from 1 – 10, 1 being mild discomfort, 10 being extreme.

Practice this visualization daily along with shaking out any irritation or clearing specific anxieties that occur when you interact with them.

(Visualization #15,*The Jell-O Wall: Moving Beyond Anxiety And Worry*, Day 1)

Rate your sense of discomfort in the relationship once more at the end of the 5-day period.

DAY 8

PRACTICAL INTUITION

Leaders trust their guts. Intuition is one of those good words that has gotten a bad rap. For some reason, intuition has become a 'soft' notion. Garbage! Intuition is the new physics. It's an Einsteinian, seven-sense, practical way to make tough decisions. Bottom line... The crazier the times are, the more important it is for leaders to develop and to trust their intuition.

Tom Peters

Learning to use one's intuition is crucial for Good Work, particularly when crucial decisions must be made. Intuition can tell you when well meaning advice is off the mark, warn you when to take care, and, most exciting of all, it can sense positive opportunities coming your way. Your intuitive capacity is the ultimate tool for keeping you on track to your dreams because it can be used to cut through a mass of data to show you which is most useful for a current project.

Intuition is also the source of Good Work's spontaneous creativity: those genius moments when you know in a flash exactly what will suit that customer's needs perfectly, or how to rearrange one small element of a design to greatly improve its efficiency or aesthetic appeal. Intuition breaks through the restrictions that left-brain logic places upon your thought processes.

Unfortunately, however, in a highly rationalist world, relying on intuition has a bad rap. But often for good reasons.

People who claim to have psychic talents can be irresponsible and ungrounded. A woman I once knew had a successful business but becoming weary of it decided to ask her higher self what she should do instead. The answer was 'Go North.' She was very excited. She let her house, sold her business and relocated without considering how the move would affect her whole life. When she arrived at her destination she discovered that her body hated the climate, her emotional self was distressed that she had left friends and family behind, and she had no idea where her new work could actually be found!

This is an example of the flakey behaviour of people that is blamed on intuition, but more accurately is a sign of their inability to marry intuition with practical considerations.

Even when people are more grounded, gut instincts, psychic flashes and hunches are mysterious, and can only be vindicated in retrospect; most people have little way of determining whether a hunch is genuine guidance or simply a wishful or fantastical thought. Intuition seems random, uncontrollable and unreliable; therefore, spiritual guidance from the higher self is too dubious to be taken seriously.

However, if you are to use your intuition effectively, both skepticism and unbalanced faith have to be set aside. Accepting its mystery and yet ensuring your intuition remains practical and responsible is a skill that Good Workers need. In short, you must learn how to harness and evaluate intuitive insights appropriately.

Using Intuition Effectively

Intuitions arise from the higher self, that part of the brain that has access to invisible or information beyond one's conscious or prior learning. Higher self insights can make your work easier, more powerful or more distinctive. You can learn to call on your higher self at will, although it requires practice and common sense.

In practical terms, using the higher self in a grounded way means that you:

1. Know exactly what information you want to receive from your higher self for specific situations;
2. Are able to sense when you are connected to/listening to the higher self;
3. Can balance intuitive information with common sense practicalities when making decisions.

The aim of the following exercises is to illustrate these requirements, and to encourage a balanced approach to intuition.

VISUALIZATION #21
Sensing The Energy Of The Higher Self

In this visualization you learn to recognize when your body and mind are aligned with your higher self's energetic frequencies. Although intuition seems to be the result of being out of the body, the ability to bring higher self energy into the *whole* physicality is essential for authentic and useful communication. We recommend that you practice this technique even if you know a different way of gathering intuitive insights; it guarantees that the body is connected to the higher self, not just your imagination or feeling state.

Stage 1: Preparation

Your position and environment are important for this practice. If you are uncomfortable, it is hard to let your mind slip into the light, soft relaxation that helps you sense your higher self.

- ⊙ Begin your practice by finding a warm space to sit in where you will not be interrupted for at least 15 minutes.
- ⊙ Make sure that you have cleared any inner disturbance before this practice, such as entanglement with others' emotions, anxiety or anger.
- ⊙ Make sure your spine is straight and well supported.
- ⊙ Place your legs comfortably apart with feet on the ground.
- ⊙ Let your hands rest easily on your thighs.

Stage 2: The Practice

1. Close your eyes softly. Breathe deeply. Relax as you breathe out. Return to normal breathing.
2. Pretend that you are asking your higher self to help you. It does not matter if you have no understanding of what this energy is. It understands you.
3. Drop all tension in the body.
4. Take your focus to your feet, legs, and then hips. Release all need to hold yourself tight against life.
5. Focus on the jaw and head. Drop all tension there, relaxing completely. Feel the relief as you let the chair take the weight of your body. Feel heavy.
6. Imagine looking down at your feet. Pooled around your feet is a warm, clear, colored light. The color you sense feels safe and relaxing.
7. Put one hand below the navel as close to your pubic bone as possible. Focus your attention on the tailbone. Imagine the warm, clear light is also in your hand.
8. Using your in-breath to assist you, imagine the light with its warmth and safety moving up through your body from the tailbone. On the out-breath, release any extra tension.
9. Imagine yourself filled with this light. Rest with this imagining for a moment. Experience it.
10. Take your other hand and place it on the top of your head.
11. Imagine, around the top of your head, another different colored pool of warm, clear light. Imagine this new color is also safe and relaxing. Feel your hand filled with this light. (You may now take your hand away if you wish.)

12. Using your breath to move the energy, let the light move down through the top of your head, down through your whole body, filling you with this warmth.
13. The two colored lights mix and move through your body, each color adding to the other. They grow more beautiful, brighter, and stronger.
14. Imagine you are glowing: radiating these mingling lights. Feel a greater sense of your self: a radiant, more expansive you. Add more warmth and color. Feel yourself radiate even more.
15. You are now filled with the energy of your higher self. Stay with this feeling until you sense that your body and mind have registered it. Return your awareness to the room. Rest. Open your eyes when you are ready.

Follow Through Options

Option #1

VISUALIZATION #22

Observing How Your Higher Self Helps You In Daily Life

Your intuition is always online if you wish it to be. You don't have to do a visualization or be in meditation to connect to it. However, the way that the higher self speaks in everyday situations varies from person to person, and to cultivate it requires observation of its preferred avenues. Some messages come through reading, some through other people's comments, some through dreams or synchronicities.

To explore how the higher self works with you in everyday life, set yourself a simple question in regards to a work issue, and continue as follows.

1. Go to *The Inner Garden Of Serenity And Well-Being* (Visualization #1, How To Use This Book).
2. Relax fully. Place your hand over your heart.
3. Imagine that you invite into your garden a wise person who represents your higher self in human form.
4. Ask your question. Pretend that the answer is coming to you in the form of energy flowing from the wise person and being drawn into your body.
5. Take a little time to absorb this energy - even if you don't feel it!
6. Keep your attention on your heart, and stay open to the idea that the answer is settling there. (You may even sense it immediately but do not be concerned if you do not because that is not the aim of this technique, which is simply to feel your higher self energy connecting to a question.)
7. Open your eyes when you are ready.
8. Now stay alert to the higher self's message coming to you over the next 24 - 36 hours. A piece of information will attract your attention or resonate with you within that timeframe. It will have an 'aha' quality to it. Notice the specific avenue the higher self uses to deliver it to you because this avenue is one that your higher self prefers to use.

Note carefully: Information from the higher self is always kind, helpful and loving. If, using this visualization, a message comes that suggests you should do something harmful or risky, or will hurt another person, it is not a higher self communication - ever!

Option #2

TECHNIQUE #12

Balancing Conscious And Intuitive Information For Grounded Decisions

This is an advanced technique to be used only when you are thoroughly familiar with Option 1. Read the instructions over several times before following them. It is especially important that you understand Steps 8 and 9.

1. This exercise assists you to decide whether you will or will not act on a possibility *that you have already researched and thought about.* The mental preparation makes certain that your personality self has all the information it needs.
2. Write out the question you want to ask your higher self in a simple short question. Example: Should I apply for the advertised job in X company? Note carefully: The technique cannot be successfully applied to choose between two alternative courses of action, e.g., Should I apply for X or Y company?
3. On an A4 sheet of paper, draw up 2 columns, headed Advantages and Disadvantages.

4. In the Advantages column, list all the reasons a proposed course of action would be good from three perspectives: logical, emotional and bodily welfare. For examples, I will improve my CV by having experience in X company so that I can get better paid jobs in the future (mental logic); I would enjoy working more closely with customers as X's job description indicates (emotional pleasure); X is very close to home so I would be less tired by travelling (bodily welfare).
5. In the Disadvantages column, list all the logical, emotional and bodily disadvantages. Examples: I don't have all the qualifications to be sure I will be considered for X job (logic); I will feel nervous stepping into unfamiliar demands (emotional concern); the job requires willingness to put in overtime. That would be exhausting (bodily stress).
6. You will now have two lists to compare the advantages and disadvantages of applying for this job from the point of view of your human personality. It is likely that a preferred course of action will now be clear to you. (If there is no clear result, continue adding advantages and disadvantages until the preference is revealed.) You now have a decision based on your conscious processes.
7. But what does your higher self think? To find out your higher self's attitude, start by taking out a coin to 'decide' the answer by flipping it. Assign Heads to the preferred course of action for your personality self, e.g., I will take the job while Tails will indicate that you will not.
8. *Now for the really important part!* First, close your eyes and ask your higher self to provide you with an intuitive answer.

Pretend you can sense its energy as you learned to do in Visualization #21.

9. Flip the coin, keeping your attention on your body. When the coin comes down, notice your body's response to the answer *immediately*. Do not allow yourself to think! If it comes down heads and you feel a rush of pleasure or relief, then your higher self is in agreement with your personality self's logic; if it comes down heads and you feel physical discomfort, your consciously preferred course of action should be reconsidered. (If the coin shows Tails, again notice your body response, and apply the same feeling criteria.)

Note carefully: You should not necessarily act on the intuitive information provided by this exercise even if it does align with your personality's assessment after giving it further thought. The exercise is intended to teach you how to *feel* an intuitive response; that may not be your final decision. For example, upon second thoughts you might realize you are not yet ready to make a move because your current job is still giving you useful experience. *Your higher self's perspective does not dictate the action you should or must take.* The higher self is a valuable source of extra information to be used to make the fully rounded decisions that your true self requires for Good Work. It is not, despite the word higher, the ultimate authority.

DAY 9

CONSCIOUSLY HARNESSING THE ENERGY OF LOVE

'The gods do many things. Some are ordinary. Some are miraculous. But one thing should always be recalled, Blade of Grass: they do all things using human hands, never their own.'

Nury Vittachi, *The Feng Shui Detective goes South*[1]

This book is about bringing more love to yourself and others through the work you do. The more you can harness love at every point, the more your work will become Good. In today's exploration, we show you a technique you can use to direct the energy of love into specific situations.

But love is a confusing word. It is fraught with misunderstanding because it is associated with feeling states such as affection, tenderness or passion, or actions that relate to caring and generosity. Yet love as energy is much more encompassing than these tangible and practical manifestations of it. It is a force that can be called upon to transform and evolve every aspect of life distorted by ignorance or distress. Love also generates more of itself: it is evolutionary.

1 Nury Vittachi, *The Feng Shui Detective goes South*, Felony & Mayhem, 2010

By broadening your understanding of love as energy, you can harness it to uplift and support all your work projects, whether or not you regard them as Good.

Love As Energy

Love energy is a generic term for all those frequencies that assist living things to survive, evolve and to participate in the many delights that life brings. Like electricity, the frequencies of love are unseen but they generate light, warmth, comfort and pleasure.

Those who value their spirituality are, in essence, valuing the fundamental energy of love. Some see that energy as flowing directly from God or The Source; others see it as being created by human endeavor. Both are correct. Universal or soul love flows through human channels to transform love energy into the many forms that bring well-being and enjoyment to earthly existence.

Love In Tangible And Unassuming Forms

Love in tangible form is found everywhere: in clear water that refreshes, in the fire that warms, and in the beauty of changing seasons. This kind of love is understood as God's gift: it is not earned. However, tangible love is also manifested in the billions of products and humble daily services that people create to make life better in some way.

Thus, all workers are part of the creation of an enormous web of multi-faceted love that spans time and space, even if they are unaware of it, and even if they do not particularly like their job. Only when an individual intentionally acts with malice does work utterly fail the love test.

Reflection

Take your attention to something close by as you read these words: your computer, the chair you sit in, or a cup of coffee. Consider in what ways your life would be impacted if you did not have access to that item.

Now think of every type of work that was needed to bring it to you. The range of love that work brings to each moment of our day is amazing.

Harnessing The Power Of Love As Energy

Beyond giving and receiving love unconsciously as we do every day, there is also the possibility of harnessing the energy of love consciously.

Faced with difficult situations, a Good Worker needs to be able to send love in a stronger, purer form than that which permeates the problematic situation.

Love as energy is diluted by the presence of discordant energies. If you are affected by contaminants such as self-pity, self-righteousness, obligation, manipulation, jealousy, anxieties and repressed anger, the strength of your ability to harness love energy is weakened by those non-love energies. Therefore, if you are to give and receive love to the degree you want, you must first be aware of these contaminants and clear them. Once that is done, you will be able to stream a higher form of love energy into specific situations to cleanse and uplift those negative influences over which you have no direct control.

The following visualization illustrates how to do this. It will not necessarily create instant magic – although we have known it to do so – but each time you practice it you will be lifting accumulated negativity just a little bit until improvement is noticeable.

VISUALIZATION #23
Consciously Harnessing Love Energy To Uplift Any Work Situation

The following visualization is a means of using the energy of love to improve any aspect of your life. In this case, you use it specifically for work issues, but of course you can use it for purely personal situations.

Stage 1 primes your brain for the main visualization that follows. It is important that you are calm before you practice it. If necessary, clear any anxiety by using Visualization #15, *The Jell-O Wall*, Day 1, A 10-Day Course In Making Daily Work Good, or if you are irritable, rid the body of its angry feelings by vigorously shaking them out.

Stage 1

1. Get yourself a pen and paper. Find a comfortable place to sit where you won't be disturbed.
2. On one side of the paper, list the difficult work situation or a project you want to see flourish. If you would like, imagine the people involved, and write their names down too.
3. Now draw to mind and list as many of the various things you love and enjoy about life that you can: they do not necessarily have to have anything to do with your job or the project.
4. It is very important that you put your feelings as well as your thoughts into creating this list. Spend as much time as you like dreaming, feeling and thinking of all your loves and enjoyments, past and present.

5. If you take a break here, read over your lists to re-engage your thoughts and feelings before moving to Stage 2.

Stage 2

1. Go into your Inner Garden of Serenity and Well-Being (Visualization #1, How To Use This Book.)
2. Imagine that you draw a circle upon the ground around you: your circle of power. Give yourself comfortable space as you stand in the middle of it.
3. Bring to mind the difficult situation you are currently experiencing, or the project you would like to see flourish.[2]
4. Place this difficult situation, people or project outside your circle of power within a glass container, like a large aquarium.
5. Take your awareness back to yourself standing in the centre of your circle. Feel your feet on the soft, warm surface and recall all those things you love and enjoy about life from your list. Of course, you can imaginatively add more.
6. Take your time to bring the experiences into this moment by fully feeling the pleasure of each one.
7. Put your hands over your heart, and with these warm thoughts and feelings, imagine the muscles around your chest relaxing. Your face relaxes, too, until you maybe want to smile. Imagine the heart feels fuller, somehow stronger. Your fears drop away. Breathe and enjoy the love you are now consciously creating. Take a moment to enjoy this.

---

2 You can also apply this technique to a problem that you have had in the past but do not wish to have again.

8. As you breathe in, imagine this love fills you up until it overflows.
9. As you breathe out, send the overflowing love outward to that work situation, people or project on the outside of your circle. Imagine this well-being flowing over and around them, providing comfort and upliftment. If it is a project you want to see flourish, imagine this well-being providing it with vitality and nourishment.
10. Take your time to fully imagine that difficult situation relaxing and the people smiling, enjoying these gifts of well-being and love. Exit when you feel completed.

Follow Through Option

Practice Stage 2 as part of your inner work twice a week for a month. Monitor the effects by observing changes in the atmosphere at work. Sensitive people will be calmed by the increased love energy.

DAY 10

LETTING GO: THE ART OF TRUST

This is love: to fly toward a secret sky,
to cause a hundred veils to fall each moment.
First to let go of life. Finally, to take a step without feet.

Rumi

Good Workers work well because their natural aptitudes are engaged. They also want their projects, large or small, to have positive impact. They are committed to their work being the best it can be given their level of experience and understanding because the heart of the true self is in it. In short, they leave no stone unturned in their quest to realize their dreams for their work.

However, this intense commitment has its own risks. Work exists in a matrix of numerous factors beyond the direct control of the single person whose dream is giving direction to it. Therefore, Good Workers are liable to become distressed when obstacles beyond their sphere of influence regularly thwart their goals. They grow impatient. The longer there is a delay, the more anxious they become. They wonder if they have done enough, if they have missed some essential element. They over work details, or become resigned to disappointment. Whatever the response, they lose the belief that life and their spirit will find a way for their work to have the success they desire.

When delay or apparently insurmountable obstacles plague you, it is time to throw your dream like a kite into the Universe to let the winds of spirit take it high above the logic of coalface realities. It is time for genuine spiritual trust because only spirit knows how and when a particular work will find its niche in life. And only truly trusting in this grander design offers the serenity that allows you to have patience and keep your faith strong.

A friend from long ago told me how he yearned to become a recognized actor. He spent a lot of money investing in training and auditioned regularly for various productions in which he won small parts. But his acting career did not really take off. He had to rely on his work as a roofing contractor for his income. However, this man was deeply convinced that his soul and spirit were his real agents.

He explained it to me this way: 'I used to sit on a roof looking out over whatever was going on below me. I enjoyed watching the interesting things I saw there. I kind of accepted that life was giving me what I wanted anyway. But then I would look to the horizon and imagine that a big acting job was flowing from it to me.

The months turned into three years. Then, one day, I was up on a roof and my wife phoned me with the news that a Hollywood director had seen me in a film and wanted to offer me a part. That was how I ended up in big films.'

As it turned out, my friend found that living in the United States was hard on his family. He was not particularly upset about this. He had achieved his dream and realized that it was time to turn his creative nature to new ventures: he became a teacher and poet.

This, then, is the last and often most difficult lesson for Good Work:

letting go and letting God. It is a process, but not one born of desperation or resignation: it is a process in which you do what you can in practical ways and you keep dreaming. But at the same time you find joy in life as it is. You do not cling to the form in which your dreams will come true, but let new paths open as they will.

The next two visualizations promote an inner trust that matters beyond your control will be resolved either by the passage of time or by specifically asking for your higher self's assistance.

VISUALIZATION #24
Trusting The Processes Of Life

This visualization helps you to trust that the process of life itself will support your Good Work.

At times of emotional expansion or stretch, you may find that, despite other inner work to clear anxiety, you hang on to out-dated or restricted forms of thinking or chronic patterns of worry. These pessimistic mental and emotional attitudes often prevent a new stage of Good Work from unfolding.

1. Begin by identifying the stagnant situation, anxiety or negative expectation that is standing in the way of a more trusting attitude to life. For example, you might believe that a Good Work project will not progress without you micro-managing it, or you obsessively worry that failures of the past will repeat themselves.

2. Relax and call in your higher self's energy as you experienced in Visualization #21, *Sensing The Energy Of The Higher Self*, Day 8.
3. Imagine yourself sitting beside a broad, fast-flowing river. You see it winding its way past you and into the far distance. This is the river of life.
4. In the middle of the river is a large rock. The rock represents your stuck attitude or worry.
5. Allow yourself to wade into the water and feel it dragging at your body, trying to sweep you off your feet.
6. Make your way to the rock. Grab hold of it tightly to stop yourself floating away. Sense how tightly you are holding on. The river of life is moving on without you.
7. Notice that there are steps in the rock that allow you to climb to the top. Up here the rock feels sharp beneath your feet and no matter how you move you cannot find a comfortable place to stand.
8. Ask your higher self to surround the rock, and to throw over it a blanket of pure light.
9. Sense yourself relaxing as the light flows over the rock. You can let go now. You see the light dissolving the rock entirely.
10. Suddenly you are floating safely and freely down the stream.
11. The current naturally and easily changes into a beautiful pool. It is rich with life: water lilies, birds, plants and shady trees growing at its edges. Sense it fully. Allow the pool to become what most pleases you. Rest there and absorb the life around you.
12. You are enjoying life's processes and trusting them. Exit the visualization when you are rested and ready to leave.

In the next visualization, you give the progress of your project or the resolution of problems over to the care of your higher self. You are practicing trust in the power of spirit to help you.

VISUALIZATION #25
Handing Your Projects And Problems Over To Your Higher Self

Human life is often experienced as a solitary journey without support; the idea that you can give your problems over to spirit seems, especially for skeptics and rationalists, an airy-fairy nonsense. But, it is a spiritual truth that your higher self has the job of bringing you what you want, which it does by putting you in the path of unexpected opportunities or smoothing an otherwise rocky road.

When you have done all you can to achieve a goal, the next step is to hand the project over to spirit.

When practicing this visualization, concentrate on what it is you want to create positively. If you find yourself desiring negative experiences for yourself or others, we suggest you first clear these feelings thoroughly.

Once you have completed the visualization, make sure you truly let go of worrying about it. Focus on where you can enjoy life as it is.

1. Go to *The Inner Garden Of Serenity And Well-Being* (Visualization #1, How To Use This Book) and *Anchor The Light* (Visualization #4, Chapter 5).

2. Call in your higher self to assist you. Imagine it standing in front of you as a person. Also invite in all those unknown people who will help to bring your desire to you.
3. Begin by telling your higher self what it is you want. The thoughts, feelings, words, or mental pictures move out from you. Take your time. Relax.
4. These imaginings form a package. (Be creative here. Allow your imagination to be guided by your higher self to form the most suitable container.)
5. Imagine now that the unknown helpers hold out their hands and gently take the container. They know exactly what to do with it. You may experience a change in the look of the container.
6. Breathe deeply. Relax.
7. At your feet a pot appears. It contains a glowing, granular substance. Put your hand in to it and feel the wonderful texture. This light substance is for cleansing your reality so you can see and feel with clarity to bring opportunities to you.
8. Throw the light substance over and around yourself. Absorb this energy until you feel completed and then exit the visualization.

PART SIX

YES BUTS ...

Doubt everything or believe everything:
these are two equally convenient strategies.
With either we dispense with the need for reflection.

Henri Poincare

The Good Work Book proposes that you add incomparable value to the world when you express and support the authenticity of your true self in your work. We believe that to learn how to do this with ease and effectiveness is a grand spiritual purpose; the love held within your soul's gifts contributes the best of you to something bigger than yourself, whether you conceive that bigger field to be service to individuals, God, humanity, the planet, or an aspect of life you enjoy.

However, this proposition is a radical one because the current social and economic paradigms are such that there are many forces that weigh against spiritually orientated self-expression at work. It is, therefore, natural that as a reader you may have some serious doubts about the feasibility of creating your own Good Work. It is true that many people will find Good Work hard to achieve in their major income earning activities.

However, there is space in everyone's lives for some Good Work somewhere, and each time that occurs more true self love is injected into human affairs. Therefore, we only ask that you stay open to finding some of the propositions and techniques presented here as worthy of consideration.

Some answers to the most common objections to the possibility of making work Good are provided in Part 6. If you have comments or queries beyond these, you may like to contact us at www.thegoodworkbook.com.

OBJECTION #1

THE SAD STATE OF MY BANK ACCOUNT

One of the most commonly offered reasons for being unable to commit to the search for Good Work is lack of money. People say, 'Look, what you say makes sense, but I have a mortgage to service. I can barely pay the bills as they are. I can't create Good Work because I can't afford it.'

It is certainly true that financial considerations have to be taken into account if you plan major change to your working life. Furthermore, when you take a new direction we would certainly not suggest that you should ignore practical matters on the theory that if you do what you love, the money will come. This is a half-truth only. The laws that govern wealth creation stand separate from those that govern your aptitude and passion for particular kinds of work. This is always true except for the few who are gifted with working with money as a true self purpose.

Reaching financial goals is an entirely different endeavor from the process of turning a job into Good Work. This means that if you wish to create financial security or freedom, learning ways to increase your income, using what money you have better, or growing your assets cannot be avoided.

Nevertheless, whether you have little money or lots, pleasure in work can always be improved by the methods offered in this book. And that, in itself, will make your life feel richer.

But what if you have a form of Good Work that you love but it does not make enough money, and you wish it to do so? There is good news and bad in relation to this question.

The bad news is that you might need to accept that your Good Work will always need to be supplemented by other income-earning activities, which will be less to your liking.

The good news is that every profession can point to individuals who find ways to make a good living from it, even if the majority does not. The difference between those who are likely to create money from Good Work and those who will struggle depends on the degree to which the person has an easy relationship to money itself.

Unfortunately, a comfortable relationship to money is often difficult to develop because there are many powerful collective attitudes attached to it that are thoroughly unpleasant: anxiety, guilt, resentment, control, fears of lack, and fears of greed. Money and fear are, regrettably, inextricably linked in social consciousness. Therefore, if you are to disentangle from your own connection to such negativity, you will need to make it a focus of your personal growth; make money a friend and not an enemy of love.

It is not our purpose to discuss the principles of improving your money consciousness in depth here. However, if you wish to have an easier relationship to money, begin by creating a dream for how you will use it based on what you know from experience would give you, not just relief from anxiety, but true joy.

Above all identify and change your beliefs about powerlessness in relation to financial matters. Clear all your anxieties regularly as they come up. (You will do that often!) The techniques supplied in earlier sections are basic ones but they can take you a long way to enlighten your money consciousness.

VISUALIZATION #26
Cultivating A Money Garden

The following visualization, which depends on you being familiar with earlier visualizations, is an excellent method of *maintaining* positive attitudes to money. It does not clear negative beliefs and fears, which must be cleared by selecting a relevant brain change technique. (See Index of Visualizations and Techniques.)

1. Go to *The Inner Garden Of Serenity And Well-Being* (Visualization #1, How To Use This Book). Invite a person who you imagine works easily with money to join you.
2. Sit and rest in your garden for a moment, letting yourself fully relax.
3. Imagine that you give your current concerns about finances over to your moneyed friend in a document file.
4. Walk towards a hedge or wall with a door or gate that screens a special money garden from the rest of your garden.
5. Quickly open the gate and glimpse what your garden looks like today: it will change often because money energy changes quickly.
6. Step into the garden and see what needs to be done today: e.g., clearing debris, cutting new paths, planting, fertilizing, watering, harvesting, etc. Imagine you carry out these tasks.
7. Now step into the centre of your money garden and create a circle of power.

8. Bring your money friend into the circle and feel them with you.
9. *Anchor The Light* (Visualization #4, Chapter 5). Radiate your light into your circle of power fully, and then into the whole money garden.
10. Step into the garden to see what it now looks like. You may sense that you need to do a little more adjustment to it.
11. Exit the visualization when you feel it is right to do so.

Optional Extra

You may wish to add to this visualization by opening gates from your garden to create money avenues from the outer world. If you choose this option, absorb the incoming money energy and then let it go back to the world, creating a circulation of receiving and giving.

OBJECTION #2

TIME POVERTY

We are not going to pretend that transforming work into Good Work doesn't take time. It does. At the very least, you need time for the inner work that transforms negative responses into Good Work attitudes. However, despite the fact that visualizations only take 5 to 15 minutes per day, beginners sometimes procrastinate claiming they don't have enough time for them. This resistance is born out of self-sabotaging attitudes and habits that need to be cleared.

As you read the checklist below, consider which of these are relevant to any resistance you might have for setting aside time to create Good Work.

Compliance with a social judgment that personal growth is not important to earning a living

When people are unwilling to prioritize time for personal growth it is often because they don't see self-reflection as useful or relevant to solving the immediate pressures of earning a living.

This attitude is legitimized by the 24/7 365-day economy made possible by advances in communication technologies. The rhythm of the past with its regular times for religious observance has largely broken down in Westernized urban environments. These moments were dedicated to spiritual connection and, to some extent, to self-reflection. However, the secular world of the twentieth century abandoned these rituals as being superfluous to 'real life' while self-reflection was often stigmatized as being the preferred activity of introverted navel-gazers, aka losers. Top performing athletes know otherwise; they know that their mental and emotional attitudes are critical to success.

Unconscious avoidance of the possible consequences of self-reflection

For some individuals, there is a fear that self-reflection will bring up unpleasant emotions, experiences, or require uncomfortable reassessment of habitual positions.

This fear is fuelled by a commonly held assumption that self-reflection is only necessary for those who are emotionally or mentally disturbed, and society's fringe dwellers such as artists and mystics. It is simply not true: anyone who wants to be happy must work out which of their attitudes makes them unhappy, and set about changing them.

Time slips away

In this case a person, usually a right brain orientated personality, knows they have enough time but somehow it slips from under them so that life skills regarded as less pressing, such as building balance into their working lives or committing to time management, are never developed.

This problem is often a matter of a Sky individual's lack of a natural ability to contain work activities via schedules, planners and to do lists that cover Wheel of Life Balance necessities (Chapter 8). They prefer dreaminess and activities that create a sense of freedom from restrictions and emotional pressures. Containment feels uncomfortable. Even when a task must be addressed, the Sky individual will put it off for another more appealing moment – which never comes.

Lack of willingness to prioritize tasks or take shortcuts.

Perfectionism about one's tasks is another reason for not allowing enough time for self-care. In this case, near enough is never good enough.

One client I knew had a severely disabled teenage son. She had a huge workload as a result of having to care for him and the rest of her family. When I questioned her on the time it took for her to do various tasks I learned that she hand-washed his nappies. This was quite unnecessary as she had a washing machine, but she felt that it was a sign of being lazy and less than loving if she did not hand-wash. She was extremely resistant to the idea of reducing her time on this task because she had become a perfectionist whose fear that she was not a good mother was preventing her finding creative ways to ease her load.

Skepticism that brain change techniques will really work

Neuroscience is new to humanity. Unfamiliarity breeds hesitation to commit to visualizations, but this reluctance is also partly due to a fear that changing brain pathways will be difficult or scary. However, as you have probably read some of the visualizations by now, you will already have proof of the falsity of these assumptions. None of the visualizations can cause harm, though they will be ineffective without regular practice.

The real source of prejudgment will be an inner saboteur who generally prefers that you do nothing than try something to advance yourself.

If you think you may be driving your life under its influence, draw a little figure to represent it, or look for an illustration of a monster or evil character that is determined to get in the way of your attempts to improve your life. Then, go to your Inner Garden of Serenity and Well-Being (Visualization #1, How To Use This Book). Put your saboteur into a jar, cork it and hand it over to your higher self with firm instructions to banish it every time you decide to do some inner work.

Regrettably, the inner saboteur will pop up again regularly. Keep a reminder to banish it somewhere you will easily see it. (Of course, it will tell you that last suggestion was not worth remembering!)

Solutions To Time Poverty

The easiest solution to not having enough time for personal growth is simply to play with this book, reading any visualization that appeals at any time that suits you for just five minutes. (It's a great time-filler for insomniacs.)

If you are a more logical type, decide which of the following processes would be useful to clear your fear/belief that you don't have enough time to do the inner work necessary for Good Work.

1. Change a (negative) mental belief or skepticism about personal work or brain change techniques (Visualization #3, *Changing A Mental Belief*, Chapter 2).
2. Disentangle from those who would pooh-pooh your desire to improve your work via personal growth (Visualization #20, *Disentangling From The Energetic Impact Of Other People*, Day 7).
3. Clear fears of inner work, self-evaluation or anything else about time-related issues that affect you (Visualization #15, *The Jell-O Wall: Moving Beyond Anxiety And Worry*, Day 1).
4. If you think you are a right brain procrastinator, *Brain Balancing Exercise No. 1* (Visualization #12A, Chapter 18) will begin the process of change but taking action to set and observe time limits is also important. Use Visualization #13, *Releasing Resistance And Procrastination*, Chapter 19 whenever you find you are not using time properly by getting on with tasks that need immediate attention.

OBJECTION #3

MY OVERCROWDED LIFE

Creating Good Work is not just about making your job pleasant and rewarding. It is about having a life that addresses the activities of the Wheel of Life in a balanced way (Chapter 8), but also gives time and space for you alone.

Time out lets your mind go free of all connections to the world. It may be judged as pointless dreaming or regrettable withdrawnness, but in reality time out takes you away from the programs, external and internal, that govern your normal life so that you can rebalance your brain. Unlike mundane activities, it has no function other than surrendering to the rhythms of your own being. It occurs when you leaf through a book of recipes or DIY projects with the vague idea that you might try one of them out. You do it just for the pleasure of sifting through images and ideas. You don't really intend to act, but allow yourself to drift through possibilities. When you come out of such moments there is an indefinable sense of having been nourished.

Giving yourself space is just as important. This happens when you step away from your normal environment to a place where you can rest, focus on yourself or do your own thing away from the physical presence of any other person.

However, a commitment to making space is often rejected outright because it looks suspiciously like self-centredness or laziness. You are not being obviously productive, and others sense that you have slipped away from connection with them. Either they (usually left-brainers) or you yourself will indulge in guilt trips: Why don't you do something useful? Why haven't you phoned me? Are you okay? You don't seem your usual self, etc.

The general implication is that you don't deserve to have any space for yourself but should always fill your life with tangible achievements or social interaction.

When the need for space is not acknowledged or supported, many people let their lives become swallowed by the crowd. They fill non-work time with days crammed with personally meaningless social events or draining obligations.

Of course, participation in relationships is an essential way of giving and receiving love. It gives great pleasure and reward. It grows self-confidence and self-esteem. But if you do not allow yourself space and time to focus on your own being, this participation ultimately becomes exhausting and self-denying.

The goal of being a loving and participating person is, counter-intuitively, undermined when the true self has no place to hang out with you and you alone. Your relationships become distorted by always pleasing others, and the underlying resentment and guilt this brings poisons the authenticity of your superficially loving connections.

Reflection

Review the past seven days. How much of your non-work time was spent in servicing the needs of others or in attending social events that your true self did not really enjoy? How often did you spend *pleasurable* time alone?

How To Create Space

Creating space is something that depends on identifying those circumstances or activities that give you a feeling of pleasurable space or time out. Therefore, you will need to experiment until you find exactly what works for you.

The more each part of the self can find space that it enjoys, the more you are likely to overcome your reluctance to leave the crowd for a while. Here are some illustrative suggestions that cover the four aspects of self.

Physical: Time alone in nature, or any kind of retreat that offers solitude and where you can't be interrupted.

Emotional: Activities that take you out of emotional connection with others, such as listening to music or private hobbies that engross you.

Mental: Finding mental activities that require no outcome other than the pleasure they bring.

Energetic: Removing yourself from the influence of others. (Visualization #20, *Disentangling From The Energetic Impact Of Other People,* Day 7) is essential if you are to avoid pressure from others' expectations. When you practice it, it is helpful to make your circle of power big enough that you can imagine it giving you a feeling of freedom. Any meditative technique that completely brings you to your centre will also assist.

OBJECTION #4

TAKING CHARGE AT WORK? YOU MUST BE JOKING!

It is rightly pointed out that workers who have freedom to take charge of how and when they work have much more opportunity to turn their job in the direction of Good Work. Less fortunate are those whose employment is hedged in by mandatory obligations, inflexible systems and external pressures that are not of their making. These jobs are the ones most likely to induce the most extreme forms of Work-is-Sorrow mentality, particularly if they have few opportunities for human interaction.

The question, therefore, is: How do I take charge of my work when my job leaves little room for Good Work adjustments?

We wish we had a magic pill to solve this problem. The human world would instantly become more grounded and compassionate if we did; we would also be billionaires. Unfortunately we do not.

It is, however, possible to reduce the mental frustration and emotional toll associated with lack of personal control. This will minimize discomfort and help to move you into a Good Work attitude of hope and grounded action.

Conscious Choice: The Get-Out-of-Jail-Card

Your first task is to break out of the psychological prison you are in. If you do not, any physical alterations will prove disappointingly ineffective because your enslaved mindset will reassert itself no matter what changes you make.

At base, all work involves restriction. The fact you have a particular job has been a choice to accept restriction: possibly a choice made unconsciously and in desperation, but nevertheless a choice. Your responses to these limitations are also subject to choice: you can work yourself into a fury, let yourself be overcome with anxiety and stress, or you can focus your emotional receptors on what is beneficial and invent ways to create greater comfort.

An honest appraisal of how you feel about the work frustrations is the starting point for making choices and decisions that will lead you into a better place in the future. Ask yourself your basic reasons for tolerating the job. Is it for the money? Is it to learn skills or gain experience to put towards future employment? Is it because, despite its restrictions, you enjoy the influence that your talents give you? Does the ability to work with or serve particular people outweigh the frustrations? Do you enjoy the certainty that a high degree of routine, supervision or guidance supplies? Or, is it simply because you are too frightened to look elsewhere because you recognize there is a degree of security in your present situation, and it suits your inner saboteur to feel sorry for yourself?

Becoming aware of the underlying reasons for tolerating your job will often reframe your attitude to it. You are likely to see that being in prison has some material benefits that you genuinely want to maintain. Those features meet needs that should not be overlooked; they may not seem very elevated in a spiritual sense or emotionally exciting but they will still be important to your true self who is also concerned for your material security.

The answers to these questions will also help decisions about the job's future: how long you intend to keep it; whether the frustration rests in the fact that you have outgrown its original purposes; and whether you might be able to negotiate changes or take on new roles that would be more aligned with your true self's preferences.

Remember, too, that restriction is not necessarily a bad thing for the true self: if you have a job where the restrictions are necessary to grow your talent or express your core potential, your true self is unlikely to resent them, though your mental or emotional aspects may find the loss of freedom irritating.

Reflection

Write down a list of the frustrations in your job. Then write down a list of its benefits mentally, emotionally and materially. Make a note of what your body enjoys about it and where it serves your passions, the exercise of your talents, and your preferences for working with certain people.

Clear Resentment

The prison-like feeling that comes with jobs that have little room for personal control is basically generated out of boredom, anger and/or anxiety.

Hold on to these emotions too long and the resulting stress will solidify into a resentment or bitterness that, not to mince my words, turns a person into an uptight, passive aggressive martyr or a self-pitying, irresponsible victim. Needless to say, that will affect all your other relationships: not something your true self will be in favor of.

Resentment is the ultimate result of anger that comes from feeling powerless. To minimize it, regularly clear your anger (Day 5), and disentangle from the people or situations that control you (Day 7). These two brain reprogramming techniques are as important as cleaning your teeth every day.

Make A Grounded Commitment To Moving Forward

If you find yourself in work that is imprisoning and it is not relieved by the recommendations here, then you must accept the possibility that, like a long-term inmate in a real prison, you have become institutionalized. When this occurs, a person is resigned to living in a dreary environment where no exits are sought. They no longer actively resent the job but they do it by rote. It's a time killer until retirement. The true self is no longer in the picture.

In this case, the inner saboteur has taken over. This is the part of you that is dead against any action that would lead you to greater happiness. The inner saboteur feeds on fears of change and those anxieties related to taking charge. It hates conscious choice and loves complacency. The only way out is to make a choice to wrest your destiny back from it.

Strategies For Escaping Prison

1. Read Objection #2 for instructions on a simple way to banish the inner saboteur.
2. Practice Visualization #9, Chapter 14 to reconnect with the energy of The Future You.
3. Clear any negative beliefs that cause fear of leaving your prison. For example, there is a job shortage so I won't find a new one (Visualization# 3, Chapter 2).
4. Define your goals for your next job (Chapter 19), but also draw a picture of the ideal job including notes showing how you are in charge of it. Creating a visual picture of the future you want provides emotional direction and upliftment.
5. Take practical steps to get a better job by updating your resume and looking through employment advertisements with the checklist of your goals for it in mind. Build a little nest egg if you think you may need it for transition.
6. Practice the following visualization.

VISUALIZATION #27
Transition To New Work

When your work has advanced to a certain level, you may want to take a new direction. At this time you will feel impatient or irritated with work that has previously been Good because it no longer allows your true self to grow. This impatience is healthy. However, don't throw the baby out with the bathwater: you need to maintain all that you have achieved so that Good Work can be explored in a different form.

This visualization will inject the energy of your previous achievements into the new. It can also be used for transition into new personal situations other than your job, such as finding more time for your family or social group.

1. Imagine you are sitting at a picnic on the edge of a lake. It is a beautiful day and all those who have benefited by your work to this point are enjoying the food, the wine, the games, and the chatter. Take time to sense this energy.
2. You look across the lake and you and your friends see a group of people on the other side of the lake, waving to you. They want you to notice them.
3. In front of you there is a jetty, jutting out into the lake. At the end of it is a small boat.
4. Walk down the jetty and ask your friends to fill the boat with the gifts of their experience with you and your work. See them and their higher selves filling the boat with colorful and beautifully wrapped gifts.

5. Climb into the boat with your whole team: your mental, emotional, physical and higher selves.
6. The winds of time and appropriate timing begin to blow your boat across the water to the waiting crowd.
7. When you reach the other shore, the crowd will rush down to the boat and you will throw out the gifts to them.
8. Hear and see their shouts of delight, wonder and surprise as they open these gifts. Notice how the noise of their excitement draws others to the cornucopia of gifts upon the shore of the lake.
9. Allow your creative imagination to unfold to suit your own situation. Enjoy the pleasure of imagining yourself in the new situation.
10. Exit the visualization when you are ready.

OBJECTION #5

MY JOB IS TOO BORING TO EVER BECOME GOOD

One of the arguments that people come up with when I talk about Good Work is that they have no interest in the job they already have or that it has so many tiresome chores attached to it that it could not possibly lead to Good Work. It is altogether too boring.

There are two methods of overcoming this objection.

New Learning

If your job is consistently tedious then it is certainly time for change that will restore your interest in working at all! This is usually accomplished by looking for employment that suits the true self better (Chapter 16), but it may also be achieved by expanding your knowledge or experience in the area of work you do. (Your higher self is always in favor of deepening your skills and/or experience so that your true self can strengthen its impact.)

New motivation can sometimes be found by reframing the purpose you are giving your job. In Chapter 17, I mentioned a young man who hated his job as a cost estimator; if he had decided that the knowledge could be put to a personal dream such as building his own home, he would no longer have been bored. In both cases, however, the decision to seek a different approach to the job that will restore interest is essential. You cannot wait for the job to magically improve without your intervention.

Bringing Lightness Into Chores

Good Work brings ease and satisfaction, but it is never an unending playtime in which you will wake up every morning with anticipation of the happy day ahead. There will inevitably be certain aspects of Good Work that are tiresome; for example, you may have a true self talent for project management but feel bored by the routines required to ensure that everyone is doing their part on time. Similarly, you may know you need to strengthen a particular skill to make it shine, but dislike the formal study required to do that.

If tedium and burden are too great, you will avoid the work required to support your Good Work or, alternatively, skimp it. Therefore, it is important to keep your true self light shining even in those moments in which tedium cannot be quickly or easily relieved. The following visualization to lighten the sense of burden around chores and obligations will help.

VISUALIZATION #28
Lightening The Load

This visualization should be applied only to those areas of work where you find chores tiresome. It massages the brain to bring color and enjoyment into work in any area where you must put in steady effort to achieve given outcomes.

It releases mental rigidity around hard tasks and in doing so brings opportunities for creating greater ease and freedom. It can be applied to unpaid work such as parenting, or daily management of your own life as well as paid employment.

1. Get yourself into a comfortable position. Close your eyes and relax, breathing to release any tension, and putting aside any concerns you might have.
2. Allow your mind to imagine an office that is dedicated to the arena of work that you find hard.
3. Let this office come to you in any form. Let it be whatever it is.
4. Enter this office and look about you. You will see a desk or bench with three trays labeled In-box, Out-box, and Think About box. The In-box has many files.
5. Set about making this office as interesting, colorful and comfortable as you can.
6. Adjust it until you feel at ease walking around it and doing the tasks. Look at the Think About box and let your mind expand to contemplate matters that are not on your list of chores. Let yourself dream a little.
7. Exit when you feel completed.
8. Return to this office from time to time, making further adjustments to keep it colorful and comfortable. See the In-box empty, the Out-box filled. Once again, let yourself enjoy the Think About box.

Follow Through Option

After you are familiar with the visualization, consciously explore ways to make chores more palatable.

If you are not able to make a small improvement, go back to the Index of Visualizations and Techniques and choose intuitively which topic will break your resistance to taking the next step on the road to Good Work.

PART SEVEN

KEEPING THE GOOD WORK GOING

So here you are! At the end of our book, and about to take the next step on your journey to Good Work. We hope you will continue to use the map we have laid out and find value and comfort in the visualizations and techniques. We would love you to leave your reviews on Amazon or post comments at www.thegoodworkbook.com.

As you will now realize, Good Work is not a destination but an ever-changing adventure that depends for its pleasure on developing those attitudes and responses that allow your true self to shine through your activities. The Good Work Book's brain-reprogramming exercises allow this to happen. They also lead to an experience of living that has great depth to it: you will not only enjoy your daily work more but you will also discover the incomparable delight of realizing that what you do is truly enriching of your own spirit as well as those who benefit by it.

Taking time out to do any one of the techniques from time to time will be beneficial. However, if you are willing to commit to a longer process of making your work Good, we leave you with one last suggestion.

The effects of inner adjustments will show up more quickly if you make a habit of maintaining your personal energy on a daily basis. The ritual below incorporates the key visualizations that maintain your connection to your true self's centre. It's so effective that many of our students have found that this practice alone makes immense improvements to all aspects of their lives, particularly relationships.

Once you have mastered the italicized visualizations, the ritual should take no longer than 5 - 7 minutes a day. Doing it even twice a week will support you.

Practicing the ritual does not circumvent the need to develop the creative balance that turns dreams into action. It is not a substitute for clearing emotional discomfort and rewriting the mental stories that prevent you finding a practical route to Good Work. Its value lies in its power to revitalize, maintain and protect your energetic field so that your true self is supported fully as you take these actions.

TECHNIQUE #13
Seven Sacred Steps Highly Effective People

(With apologies to the late Stephen Covey)

To work this ritual, clear a space in your room. Stand throughout the ritual, miming each step with firm intention.

You can also choose to invite your higher self to participate by drawing it to your awareness at the start of the ritual.

1. Imagine you are standing in *The Inner Garden Of Serenity And Well-Being*. Create a circle of power around you, eyes

open and finger pointing towards the ground. With eyes shut, adjust the size of the circle to make it comfortable.

2. *Anchor The Light.* Cross your hands over the centre of the chest and hold your attention there for about 10 seconds, imagining that the light is now mingling with your heart's energy to form a small, glowing ball.
3. Radiate this light into a full sphere all around you.
4. *Disentangle From The Energetic Impact Of Other People.* Make the disentangling feel as real as possible.
5. Throw the gift of love to the particular individuals or groups with which you have, or will have, interaction. If you prefer you can reverse this step with step 6. If you are not sure about how to send love energy, practice *Consciously Harnessing Love Energy to Uplift any Work Situation.*
6. Protect your entire energy field with an imaginary, transparent, but strong shield that reflects negativity away from you.
7. Finally, throw a ball of golden light filled with your intentions for the day as a path to step upon. You may prefer to focus on the emotional or mental states you wish to experience, e.g., calm flow, productive achievement, friendly support, playfulness, etc. Take one step on the path. Feel and adjust till it feels firm under your feet.

A Final Word For Those Who Want To Make A Difference To A Troubled World

Many readers will find the techniques we have offered here helpful in making their experience of their job better. Others will be more ambitious because they recognize that their Good Work has the capacity to make a significant impact on an aspect of society they care about.

We leave those of you who want to make a difference with a quotation from Clarissa Pinkola Estes writing at http://www.awakin.org who speaks of the power of the soul in the turbulence of a world in transition to an uncertain future. We hope it inspires you as it does us.

'One of the most calming and powerful actions you can do to intervene in a stormy world is to stand up and show your soul. Soul on deck shines like gold in dark times. The light of the soul throws sparks, can send up flares, builds signal fires ... causes proper matters to catch fire... Struggling souls catch light from other souls who are fully lit and willing to show it. If you would help to calm the tumult, this is one of the strongest things you can do.'

Suzie St George
Fiona McDougall

ACKNOWLEDGMENTS

This book owes its existence to many people, especially the regular participants in our monthly workshops in Melbourne and Daylesford. Without their support, and those of dedicated clients over many years, we could not have written it. You know who you are. Thank you, thank you, and thank you.

However, there are particular individuals whose contribution to The Good Work Book we wish to make special mention of because they have been willing to share their experiences in it. These are Jane Robotham, Alexandra Webb, Jane Knight, Kate Adams, Ryan Downey, and Steven Cincotta.

We also thank the ever-conscientious Steven for his copy editing of an early draft, Pierz and Randal Newton John, and Jan Wild of www.retirement-planning.info for their helpful comments. The wonderful artistry of Kate Adams in her preparation of the front cover lifted our hearts. Our gratitude also goes to Julie-Ann Harper and her team at Pickawoowoo Publishers for getting this book up and out there.

We also owe a debt of immense gratitude to our families and the teachers who trained us over the years.

For Suzie these are: Jeff Barlow and Daniel Weber of the Australian College of Contemporary Somatic Psychotherapy, Arny Mindell and his excellent teachers at the Process Work Institute in Portland, Oregon, Dr John R. Wilson, psychiatrist, Joy Spencer, yoga teacher par excellence, and my amazing family of writers.

For Fiona these people are: My mother, Margaret Elizabeth Wilson for always supporting my gifts, Yvonne Teoh Bource who in my early adulthood taught me to take charge of my life, and Sarah Bell for introducing me to Suzie all those years ago.

We also thank our husbands: Andrew McDougall for giving Fiona the space to flourish, and Gary Turner who glares at Suzie when she is in danger of becoming a workaholic.

Then there are those spiritual teachers, seen and unseen, who have brought so much love and guidance: Our own guides, Siramus and Tiargo, as well as Lazaris, Sanaya Roman's Orin, and Esther and Jerry Hicks whose published material we recommend.

Permissions

Our gratitude is also extended to the following people for permission to use the inspirational quotations that precede the following sections:

Day 3: *More important than the quest for certainty* ... Francois Gautier

Day 4: *Our Deepest Fear* ... Marianne Williamson, A Return to Love: Reflections on the Principles of a Course in Miracles, Harper Collins, 1992

Day 8: *Leaders trust their guts* ...Tom Peters: *Fast Company* Rule #3: Leadership Is Confusing As Hell From: Issue 44 | March 2001 | Page 124

www.ingramcontent.com/pod-product-compliance
Ingram Content Group UK Ltd.
Pitfield, Milton Keynes, MK11 3LW, UK
UKHW021433280726
14060UKWH00001BA/60

9 780994 528513